EUROPE AND THE MYSTIQUE OF ISLAM

MAXIME RODINSON

Europe and the Mystique of Islam

Translated by Roger Veinus

I.B. TAURIS

LONDON · NEW YORK

Reprinted in 2006 by I.B.Tauris & Co Ltd
6 Salem Road, London W2 4BU
175 Fifth Avenue, New York NY 10010
www.ibtauris.com

In the United States of America and Canada distributed by
Palgrave Macmillan a division of St. Martin's Press
175 Fifth Avenue, New York NY 10010

First published in 1988 by I.B.Tauris & Co Ltd
New edition published in 2002
Copyright © 1987 by the Department of Near Eastern Languages and
Civilization, University of Washington.

Sponsored by the Department of Near Eastern Languages and
Civilization and the Middle East Centre of the Henry M. Jackson
School of International Studies, University of Washington.

Originally published in French as *La fascination de l'Islam* by Librairie
François Maspero, Paris.
Copyright © 1980 by Librairie François Maspero.

A full CIP record for this book is available from the British Library.
A full CIP record is available from the Library of Congress

Library of Congress Catalog Card Number available

ISBN 1 85043 106 X
EAN 978 1 85043 106 0

Printed and bound in India by Replika Press Pvt. Ltd.

To Moïse Twersky who committed suicide in Paris in
October 1940 to escape enslavement,
Who taught me as a boy to disagree with my own people
when in the wrong,
And not to let myself be enslaved by mass opinion,
even of the righters of wrong,
A lesson only too reluctantly and too slowly learnt.

Contents

Introduction to the English Edition   *ix*

Western Views of the Muslim World   3

> The Middle Ages, 3; Toward a Less Polemical Image, 23;
> Coexistence and Reconciliation, 31; From Coexistence to
> Objectivity, 37; The Birth of Orientalism, 40; The En-
> lightenment, 45; The Nineteenth Century, 52; Challenges
> to Eurocentrism, 71

Toward a New Approach to Arab and Islamic Studies 83

> Traditional Orientalism in the Past, 85; The Present Cri-
> sis and Current Problems, 93; The Present State of the
> Craft, 99; The Continuance of the Past Impetus, 99; The-
> ologocentrism in Scholarship, 104; New Fields and Dis-
> ciplines, 107; Regional Influences in Islamic Studies, 109;
> The Modalities of Future Progress, 111; Proposals for
> Future Study, 115

Notes   *130*
Select Bibliography   *145*
Index   *153*

Introduction to the English Edition

I should, perhaps, heed the wise old adage that warns against poking one's fingers into too many pies. But that is a piece of advice I have never quite mastered and, as a result, I am at times successful at what I do, but at other times, not so successful. Here, as always, I shall have to leave it for the reader to decide.

It has always been my desire to use my expertise in my own field of specialization, first, to summarize the results of research in the field; second, to draw some general conclusions (and argue against what I consider questionable conclusions reached by others); and third, to present still broader ideas on the sociological and even philosophical levels. This is not the place to explain why my intellectual inclination has been along these lines, nor would the reader be greatly interested in such an explanation.

I have devoted a great deal of my life over many decades to the study of Islam, Islamic history, and Islamic peoples. At the same time, I have been fascinated by the way Western peoples—including scholars—have understood Islamic peoples and their history, as well as the set of ideas that are the Islamic tradition. Why? Perhaps because I was not certain that my own understanding was right. Therefore, when Joseph Schacht invited me to write a short essay on the subject to be the first chapter in a completely revised edition of *The Legacy of Islam*, which he was editing for Oxford University Press, I jumped at the opportunity. So eager was I to explore the subject that I wrote more than ninety pages when only thirty were needed. In the process, I studied and learned much that was new to me, and formed some new ideas of my own. My enthusiasm for the topic made it difficult for me to condense all of this new material and so Schacht, a very great scholar indeed, and a most modest and selfless man, generously undertook the task of both translating my original into English and reducing it to the length required. He worked with great skill, intelligence, and in perfect harmony with my ideas, even though he was not always in full agreement with them. His death in 1969 delayed publication for several years until the very learned C. E. Bosworth took over the project. He asked me to revise Schacht's translation, which I did to the best of my ability. The other contributions were made ready in similar fashion and the second edition of *The Legacy of Islam* was published in 1974.[1]

Of course, I was pleased that my research had finally been published, but I was also rather disappointed that in pruning my original text to fit the space restrictions, Schacht had been obliged to cut out lines, pages, and even whole sections. Thus, whenever an opportunity arose to present a fuller version of my ideas in lectures or short essays, I grasped it eagerly. In 1969, for example, I delivered a lecture in Cairo on the subject and a summary was published in Arabic, although the condensation was not always faithful to my ideas, and I did not have the chance to correct the final text.

I kept my original manuscript pages in French and finally, twelve years after first written, they were published in full, along with a lecture I delivered in Leiden in April 1976, by Librairie François Maspero under the title *La fascination de l'Islam*. The Leiden lecture was a kind of critical overview of the state of Arab and Islamic studies in Europe. Although the lecture was originally addressed to a European audience, this should not present difficulties for the American reader. At the very general level on which my discussion is moving, the situation described is not much different in the United States, and the necessary minor adjustments can be made quite easily. As the reader will see, I did not intend to go into great detail.

When my full text was at last available in French, it seemed that it should also be available in English. Useful as an abridgement is, and indeed, *The Legacy of Islam* version has, and continues to be, frequently cited, the complete piece is still better than the maimed one. Therefore, I was delighted when the Near Eastern Publications program of the University of Washington proposed to publish a translation of the entire *La fascination de l'Islam*. I wish to thank the publishers, their advisers, and in particular, Ellis Goldberg, who wrote the short biography of me that appears at the end of this book.

●

I should explain one or two things to the reader at this point. I have not tried to write a detailed history of the images and studies of Islam, nor was it my wish to present a kind of directory of the most eminent scholars of the field. There are already many papers and a few books, some of which are quite good, that fill that need.[2] Rather, what I intended to do was to quickly sketch a picture of the more general trends that inspired these images and studies, directed their course, and prejudiced, distorted, and colored the ideas, research, and findings. I hoped to describe succinctly what was behind the intellectual, spiritual ideas and emotions that were prompting these feelings across the whole spectrum of European society, including both the common people and the scholarly world. Scholars, and the public who rightly or wrongly admire them or merely appeal to them, are often under the delusion that they are guided at all times by rational motives or purely emotional feelings. I do not deny that reason and emotion are often present at this level, but these are not the sole factors in forming perceptions, approaches, methods, and conclusions. Scholars are *in* the world, in their world. This world of theirs cannot but influence them from all sides. In no way does it form some kind of inert backdrop on the stage where the performers are acting.

I began my studies on the relations between the East and the West, of which an examination of the factors behind their mutual views of each other was a part, long before this theme had become such an ideologically loaded issue, nay, one of the major battlefields in the ideological contest. I was myself carrying on a kind of ideological struggle. I wanted to destroy the mask of absolute neutrality and absolute purity worn by traditional scholarship. But to say that scholars *are never* perfectly neutral does not amount to saying that they *must* shun all effort toward objectivity. Nor does this mean that the best way to attain objectivity and to break the shackles of the establishment's influences is to blindly accept the ideas of the establishment's foes. Although objectivity is an admirable goal, attempting to reach it in this way simply makes a bad situation worse.

My long and painful experiences with Communism have, at least, taught me some very important lessons. We Communist intellectuals in the thirties, the forties, and even the fifties, were right, as were our predecessors, in maintaining that the workers' class of the capitalist world and the masses of the Third World were being exploited and bent to the will of others. We were also right to expose the the false impartiality of so many of the intellectuals who were controlled by the rich and powerful. Yes indeed, but we jumped too easily to the conclusion that all foes of the powerful were pure heroes, all their ideas the unalloyed truth, and all their deeds paragons of virtuous action. Now that many of us have been cured of these delusions (but at times succumbing to others), I find that others are falling into similar traps. The "good old cause" as the Cromwellian Puritans called it, was replaced by similarly presumed good new causes! Technology has advanced tremendously since Neolithic times, human societies have proliferated and become increasingly intricate, but human attitudes and passions have not changed in the slightest.

To commit oneself to a cause, to take a militant stand does not, as we dreamed, illuminate all the problems of the world, nor does it darken the entire sky as others feared. What in fact has happened is that intellectual searchlights have been trained on scenes that would otherwise have remained in the dark. But, at the same time, those very lights have cast shadows over other parts of reality.

•

I would like to take the liberty now to advertise my own design. A knowledge of Islam and the images of Islam, particularly in these times, could be an important key to the understanding of this world. There are many people who are now afraid of Islam. It is terribly true that many frightening acts are committed in the name of Islam, but these are no worse than those committed in the names of Christianity, Judaism, Freedom, and so on. Islamic peoples form a part of the world's underprivileged masses. They quite naturally long to improve their situation and will employ any means, right or wrong, to achieve that goal. This is a fundamental rule of all human nature. Many of our countrymen are therefore convinced, just as so many of our forefathers were, that the struggle against Islam is a moral obligation. It is not very difficult to discover that behind this presumed moral obligation at least some are prompted by their desire to defend (justifiably, of course) their own more or less relative welfare against the impending attacks of the underprivileged.

Conversely, many privileged people of North America and Europe became indignant over this reactionary line of defense, which resorts to equally vicious means to close all avenues of progress to the underprivileged. The virtuous among us want to share the burden of the humbled and oppressed. Some want to join the exploited, to partake wholly or partially their fate, their struggle, and even their ideas. They do not realize that to help the oppressed—a moral duty we all share—does not mean excusing all the tactics the exploited use to fight the oppressor or blindly accepting all their reasons for the causes of exploitation. Responses of this sort have caused some to become enamored of Islam and all things Islamic; a few have gone so far as to adhere to the tenets of Islam. This is the opinion of some, and everyone ought to be entitled that much. Indeed, there is much good to be found in Islamic doctrine. If, after careful study, you are convinced it is right in all matters, then why not accept it? One need only be warned that ideas must be weighed thoughtfully and adopted or rejected on their own merit. To accept a religious idea merely because its followers are sympathetic to us is, in fact, a mark of contempt for that idea and the religion of which it is a part.

Islam is, to my mind, neither the final panacea for all the evils of mankind—nowhere is there such a panacea—nor is it the Hell of the Apocalypse of today. It is both a faith and a kind of homeland. Many people are ready to die for their faith or for their homeland and they do not always have a good understanding of either that faith or the plans of the leaders of that homeland. Their readiness for martyrdom in no way decides the correctness of the tenets of their faith or the goodness of these plans or even the attractiveness of the homeland. Even less is it a guarantee of the merit of their dealings. For their faith and/or their homeland, people are commonly induced to perform splendid deeds as well as hideous crimes.

A persuasion, religious or secular, can, at most, tinge the behavior of some of its followers. Historical experience shows that it is unable to change radically the behavior of the majority over a long period by silencing the voice of their interests and of their passions. This has been so for all religions and all secular ideologies. It is equally so, of course, for Islam and has been throughout Islam's fourteen centuries of existence. Nor does anything in Islam's present situation suggest that this will change in the future. Just as there must be no discrimination against the Muslims, no defamation, no scorn, there is no obligation to applaud all their ideas and deeds.

How other peoples of different persuasions have reacted to Islam, to Muslims, to their virtues and to their crimes is exceedingly instructive. It provides a model by which foreign peoples and ideas can be understood, misunderstood, loved, hated. An awareness of the laws and principles that have made this model work in the past and present is an important tool for coping with the many ordeals from which future events, in all likelihood, will not spare us.

Maxime Rodinson
Spring 1987
Paris

EUROPE AND THE MYSTIQUE OF ISLAM

Western Views of the Muslim World

The Middle Ages

Western Christendom perceived the Muslim world as a menace long before it began to be seen as a real problem. A shift in power had occurred in the more remote regions of the East as a wild, pillaging people, non-Christian at that, overran and destroyed vast areas, removing them from Christian control. In the words of a chronicler from Burgundy writing thirty or forty years after the fact:

The race of Hagar, who are also called Saracens as the book of Orosius attests—a circumcised people who of old had lived beneath the Caucasus on the shores of the Caspian in a country known as Ercolia—this race had grown so numerous that at last they took up arms and threw themselves upon the provinces of the Emperor Heraclius.... The Saracens proceeded—as was their habit—to lay waste the provinces of the empire that had fallen to them.[1]

Under the emperors Constantine and then Constans, who followed Heraclius, "the empire suffered very great devastation at the hands of the Saracens. Having taken Jerusalem and razed other cities, they attacked upper and lower Egypt, took and plundered Alexandria, devastated and quickly occupied the whole of Roman Africa."[2] The emperor was forced to pay tribute to them.

The devastation eventually reached Spain, the coast of Italy, and Gaul, and the same wave of pillaging barbarians was always responsible. When the Anglo-Saxon monk, the Venerable Bede (673–735), revised his *Historia Ecclesiastica Gentis Anglorum* shortly before his death, he characterized these events as follows: "At this time a terrible plague of Saracens ravaged Gaul with cruel bloodshed and not long afterwards they received the due reward of their treachery in the same kingdom."[3] What he is referring to in this passage is the well-known battle of Poitiers (732) in which Charles Martel defeated the Muslims.

Apparently, few questions were raised about this people. To the Christian countries of the West, they were a plague like so many other barbarian groups. In 793, the Carolingian chronicles, erroneously attributed to Einhard, recorded the following: "two terrible afflictions arose in two different parts of the empire."[4] These were the revolt of the Saxons and the Saracen raids on Septimania (a region in what is now southern France).

The underlying attitude of the Franks toward the Muslims was basically unaffected by events. These included the alternately successful and disastrous campaigns along the Spanish border, Christian alliances with dissident Umayyad emirs, who occasionally turned to Aix-la-Chapelle for support; resistance against the raids on Gaul and against pirates off the coasts of Provence, Corsica, Sardinia, and Italy; and operations such as the landing in 828 of Boniface of Lucca in the Tunisia of the Aghlabids. According to the chroniclers, there was only a remote connection between the Saracens of the West—either the "Moors" who at times took part in European raids or the Saracens of "Africa" (Ifrīqiyā, or modern day Tunisia)—and those in Persia. This Eastern group was under the rule of the "l'amiralmummminim" (to use the most accurate spelling found in manuscripts of the period for the Arabic title "commander of the faithful"), the *rex Persarum*, or king of the Persians (elsewhere known as the *rex Sarracenorum*, or king of the Saracens).[5]

Christians had known of the Saracens, or Arabs, long before the rise of Islam, and at first the Saracens' conversion to Islam went virtually unnoticed. A fourth-century description of the world, for example, stated that the Saracens got "by bow and plunder all they required to live."[6] There was no need to know any more about them. Only scholars theorized about the origins of the name Saracen, which they believed came from Sarah, the wife of Abraham. Their other name, Agareni, however, seemed to indicate they were descended instead from Hagar, the slave girl who was driven into the desert along with Ishmael, her son by Abraham. This inconsistency did little to clarify the issue.

For obvious reasons the only group to look further than this were the Christians in Moorish Spain, the Mozarabs. Their Christian faith was seriously threatened by Muslim political domination, which exposed them to Arab cultural influences. These Spanish Christians, therefore, needed to form a more clearly defined, though perhaps not more accurate image of their rulers and their rulers' ideas. Throughout the conquered lands of the East, derogatory and abusive myths about the Saracens were widespread among the Christian and Jewish masses. But these myths were mixed with more reliable impressions based on actual daily contact. Among both the Christian apologists of the East, such as John of Damascus (700?-754), and in the West, similar efforts were made to understand Muslim thought more clearly, but with the sole objective of countering any influence it might have. Such cases of militant zeal as those of Eulogius and Alvaro of Cordova from 850 to 859, with their thirst for martyrdom, not only failed to have much effect on the Christian hierarchy or the masses, but also did nothing to advance the deeper intellectual study needed to genuinely understand the religious adversary.[7]

The Western image of the Muslim world came into sharper focus in the eleventh century. The Normans, the Hungarians, and some of the Slavs had been converted to Christianity. Thus, the Muslim world remained alone as the main enemy. Battles waged against Islam in Spain, in southern Italy, and in Sicily were no longer acts of simple resistance. The Christian advance, moving slowly and erratically, began to involve the conquered peoples themselves in greater political and even cultural interactions. What began as localized warfare grew to a mobilization of all of Europe. Europe joined the Spaniards in their struggle—the Reconquista—and the Normans marched to Italy to fight Islam. The complete fragmentation of the European states was overshadowed by the Benedictine monastic movement under the leadership of Hugh of Cluny (1024–1109), which was connected with the creation and rise of papal supremacy. The imperial Carolingian ideology centered on continental Europe gave way to the ideology of Rome, which was founded essentially on the religious values of the papacy. As a consequence of the struggle over investiture, Pope Gregory VI even humiliated Emperor Henry IV by forcing him to seek absolution at Canossa in 1077. To ensure the Christian unity so vital to the papacy, elaborate plans were drawn up and were executed uniformly under papal control. What shared adventure could be more exciting than the Reconquista, if it could be extended over the entire Mediterranean world, where the Italian commercial cities were focusing their attention and meeting with growing economic success?

The image of Islam was not drawn simply from the Crusades, as some have maintained, but rather from the Latin Christian world's gradually developing ideological unity. This produced a sharper image of the enemy's features and focused the energies of the West on the Crusades. During the eleventh century, pilgrimages to the Holy Land were becoming more numerous, better organized, and beginning to turn into armed combat against the Bedouins. The eschatological importance of Jerusalem and of the Holy Sepulchre, defiled by the infidel's presence, the purifying value of pilgrimage, and the belief that assistance was owed the humbled eastern Christians transformed these expeditions to the Holy Land into a sacred duty for the faithful.

Now that it was more consolidated and polarized, the struggle focused on a well-defined enemy with specific features, and whose general appearance was shared by all his kind. For Christian pilgrims to the Holy Land, the Saracens were little more than faceless creatures, uninteresting infidels, or incidental rulers. The mythical and satirical *Pilgrimage of Charlemagne* of the eleventh or early twelfth century, which depicts the emperor wandering through Jerusalem without the slightest contact with the city's inhabitants, is as distorted in its treatment of the East as the *Song of Roland* of about the same date, which portrays, in a style almost as fabulous, a wealthy and powerful version of Islam. In the *Song of Roland* various potentates give one another support with the aid of their many pagan bands of mercenaries, Nubians, Slavonians, Armenians, Negroes, Avars, Prussians, Huns, and Hungarians, who all share a common worship of Muhammad, Tervagant, and Apollo.[8]

In 1060, Roger of Hauteville began the reconquest of Sicily; Alfonso VI entered Toledo in 1085; and Geoffrey of

Bouillon took Jerusalem in 1099. On these three fronts, direct contacts with Muslims began to occur. A more sharply defined and accurate image of Islam began to take shape. But, for many centuries ideological rivalries within Christianity modified this image and in so doing distorted it.

In reality, Christian Europe did not, as is commonly assumed, have one, but several images of the hostile world with which it clashed. Until this point, scholars had concerned themselves for the most part with European perceptions of the Muslim religion. However, it was the Muslim world in all its aspects that confronted Christians, much to their amazement and horror. The European understanding of the Muslim world is discernible in three general areas. The Islamic world was first and foremost a hostile political and ideological system; but, it was also an utterly different civilization, and it was a remote and foreign economic sphere. With these perceptions one could harbor a wide range of reactions and questions.

The West often learned of the political divisions of the Muslim world from first-hand experience. Still, it was also understood that, for all those divisions, there was an underlying and comprehensive solidarity united behind a common ideology and faith, which could be mobilized at any moment against the Christian world. Although the Muslim states formed a hostile complex, their rivalries could occasionally be turned to the West's political advantage through temporary alliances. Christians sometimes served Muslim rulers, as the chanson de geste *Mainet* describes. There, the young Charlemagne loyally serves Galafre, the Saracen king of Toledo. Charlemagne eventually marries Galafre's daughter, who naturally converts to Christianity. In reality, episodes of this sort often did occur in Spain and the East, but nonetheless there was always a latent hostility threatening to resurface.

From a political and ideological perspective, if one compares the attitudes of Christianity toward Islam with those of Western capitalism toward communism today, the parallels are clear. In each grouping, two systems are at odds: yet within each system, a single dominant ideology unites divisive and hostile factions.

We know very little about the vision of the Muslim world held by early statesmen with their officials, informants, and spies. It must, however, have been more discerning than that of the religious ideologues or the masses. The lords of the Holy Land, with their close access to this world, would have had detailed knowledge of the internal divisions of the Muslim states, which explains the frequent alliances between some Frankish and certain Muslim leaders. This fact is exemplified in the *History* of William of Tyre (1130?-90), written for the king of Jerusalem Amalric I around 1170. Archbishop William of Tyre was a chancellor of the Kingdom of Jerusalem and was frequently in charge of diplomatic missions. In this position he was well aware of the struggle between the Sunnis and the Shī'a, the differences between the Arabs and the Turks, and the rivalries between Muslim rulers of the same ethnic origins. When Mawdūd, the Turkish atabeg of Mosul (Iraq) was assassinated in 1113 in Damascus, William observed:

[I]t was believed that Dodequins [Tughtigin], the king of Damascus, was responsible for the assassination or at least that he was in agreement with it because he [the king] feared greatly that the clever and powerful atabeg might take his kingdom from him.[9]

In these surroundings, one learned to recognize the relationships between the various powers, while perhaps unconsciously likening the situation to the European experience. Thus, the caliph (*khalīfa* in Arabic, meaning "successor") becomes the pope of the Muslims (*apostoles des*

Sarrazins) and at the same time their "sovereign prince," their "great capitain" (*chevetaine*). In the *Devision de la terre de oultre-mer*, written about 1200, Baghdad was designated the capital (*chies, chief*) of all pagandom just as Rome was the capital of all Christendom.[10]

Jean de Joinville (1224–1317), the French chronicler and translator, knew much about the organization of the Mamluk empire from direct experience.[11] For example, the peculiar Mamluk custom of entrusting the rule of the state to slaves already struck him, as the anonymous translator and continuator of William of Tyre. But this wealth of knowledge gathered by Christian statesmen in the East did not reach the rest of the world. Western missions drew from it only what was necessary for their Eastern policy. There was no particular interest in making a more detailed examination of Islamic political history, or even investigating the political quarrels among the "infidels."

Conversely, the Crusades created a huge market for a comprehensive, integral, entertaining, and satisfying image of the enemy's ideology. When seen from the outside, whole movements are invariably reduced to their bare doctrine, which outsiders take to be the substance of this broad aggregate of people on the move, with all their interests, aspirations, and passions. This is a mistake, but this is exactly what the doctrinarians of the movement intend the doctrine to mean to their faithful. But, the general public demanded an image be presented that would show the abhorrent side of Islam by depicting it in the crudest fashion possible so as to satisfy the literary taste for the marvelous so noticeable in all the works of the period. This image was composed of the most striking of the exotic traits that had impressed the Crusaders in their relations with the Muslims. Every ideological movement creates its own sacred history. Such history is used to explain a movement's appearance as the necessary antidote for the evils of the age, as drawing authority from supernatural or at least from superior forces, and as the inevitable outcome of human history. At the same time the founder of the movement is credited with extraordinary powers and is glorified occasionally to the point of deification. In the same way, any opposing movement will attempt to expose the essentially evil nature of its enemy, in so doing, rendering diabolic what is sacred for the other, especially the wicked activities of the opposition's founder.

Therefore, during the period from 1100 to 1140, Latin authors responded to the public's demand by concentrating on Muhammad's life with almost no regard for accurate details. In the words of R. W. Southern, they gave free rein to "the ignorance of triumphant imagination." Muhammad became a sorceror whose magic and deceit destroyed the Church in Africa and the East. By going on to sanction sexual promiscuity, his success was assured. Legends growing out of popular folklore, classical literature, Byzantine texts on Islam, and viciously distorted tales from Muslim sources embellished this image.[12] Southern points out that Guibert of Nogent (d. ca. 1124–30) admitted that since he had not relied on written sources, he had no way of separating fact from fiction and had only presented the *plebeia opinio*, or popular opinion. Innocently revealing the basis of all ideological criticism, he concluded that "it is safe to speak evil of one whose malignity exceeds whatever ill can be spoken."[13]

The vision found in popular works must have been, as is always the case, more influential in fashioning the image of the Muslims for posterity than that found in more reliable scholarly works. Numerous works of literature embellished that image even further. Pure fiction, whose sole purpose was to pique the reader's interest, was mixed in varying measure with distortions of Islamic beliefs, which stirred up hatred for the enemy. There were no greater examples of imaginative fancy than the chansons de geste. In them, the Muslims were accused of idolatrous worship just as the Muslims accused the Christians of "associationism" (*shirk*). Their most important idol was Muhammad, whom most of the trouvères believed to be the chief god of the Saracens. His statues were sumptuously made and colossal in size. He was credited with varying numbers of acolytes, the figure reaching seven hundred in a German work of the thirteenth century by Der Stricker.[14] According to a notion probably inspired by Christianity, it was believed that these acolytes were at times headed by a trinity of Tervagant, Apollo, and Muhammad who were worshiped in synagogues (this brought Islam even closer to the equally reprehensible Jewish faith) or in "mahomeries."[15]

An objective point of view was to be found only in a different quarter entirely, one only distantly connected to Islam, that is, in the sciences in the widest sense. Beginning in the early tenth century, and relying on a few Latin volumes saved from the wreck of ancient civilization, small groups sought to add to the treasury of theoretical knowledge about man and his world. Some knew that the Muslims had Arabic translations of the important works of classical antiquity and that complete manuals of the basic sciences were at their disposal. A few set out to find these works of scientific theory and practice, which were in the hands of the Muslims. The studies carried out in Catalonia by Gerbert of Aurillac (b. ca. 938, later to become Pope Sylvester II [999–1003]), are often referred to in this regard. From his studies in Spain, he brought back and disseminated a wealth of technical and scientific information. Muslim scientific knowledge acquired through Latin translations of Arabic works gradually began to find its way to England, Lorraine, Salerno, and above all, Spain, where contacts were readily available. The translation effort was developed and well organized in Spain after the fall in 1085 of Toledo, which was not only a great city, but one of the intellectual centers of the time.[16] No one sought in these Arab manuscripts an image of Islam or the Muslim experience, but rather an objective knowledge of the natural world. Nevertheless, some information about the purveyors of the knowledge was forthcoming. Moreover, this helped establish a close link with translators who were either converts to Christianity, Mozarabs, or Jews who had an extensive and first-hand knowledge of the Muslim world.[17]

Inevitably it was by such means as these that a more exact knowledge of the Islamic world began to reach other Europeans. This undoubtedly explains how, in the first half of the twelfth century, certain accurate observations stood out from the torrent of fabulous myths and legends that made up the popular literature about the Muslim world. There is the example of Pedro de Alfonso, a Spanish Jew who was baptized in Huesca in 1106, just four years before his death. In England he served as Henry I's physician and he went on to translate works on astronomy. But he also compiled the first work featuring any objective information about Muhammad.

It was Peter the Venerable, Abbot of Cluny (ca. 1094–1156), who first required and circulated authentic information about Islam. This remarkable achievement satisfied both the growing European intellectual interest in the sciences cultivated by the Muslims and popular curiosity about Islam. There are several reasons for the abbot's outstanding enterprise. First, in his visits to his order in Spain, he would at least have heard about the Muslim faith and the work of translators. Also, he was intent upon finding serious intellectual arguments against Christian heresies, Judaism, and Islam. His charitable manner toward "erring" souls was characteristic of the abbot's personal

style, which was evident on many other occasions as well.
Finally, he had an acute awareness of the dangers facing
the Church as it entered an age of intellectual unrest, destructive schisms, and increased dissension. The abbot's
personal code of ethics as well as his leadership of an order dedicated to preserving the Church, inspired him to
search for a way to arm the Church against such threats.
His own nature and, perhaps even the faint glimmer of a
new attitude, led him to look for weapons that would be
strong enough to combat heresies yet merciful enough to
show that Christian charity extended to anyone of good
faith. It is also quite possible that without realizing it, he
was motivated by a disinterested curiosity, which, out of
shame, he denied even to himself.

The abbot knew that his initiative would be miscon-
strued, and considering the negative reaction of Bernard
of Clairvaux (1090–1153), his friend and occasional adversary, the abbot was proved correct. In his apology, the
abbot relied on the same arguments that intellectual theorists have always used against the attacks of strict "militants." Theorists prefer, in appearance or in fact, to distance themselves from current disputes looking on them
with a certain aloofness:

> If, because the enemy is not susceptible to this kind of force, my
> project appears to be in vain, I must respond that, in the kingdom of
> a great sovereign, some acts are for defense, some for show, and still
> others for both protection and display. To defend his people, Solomon
> the Peaceful produced weaponry no one needed at the time. David
> made certain the Temple was adorned even though, at that time,
> such decoration was quite superfluous.... Nor do I think my efforts
> should be regarded as pointless. If they do not lead to the conversion
> of the Muslims, they will at least inspire the learned to sustain the
> weaker of the community who are so easily upset by minor events.[18]

In Spain, Peter the Venerable financed a team of translators. An Englishman, Robert of Ketton, finished a trans-

lation of the Qur'ān in 1143. The group translated a series
of Arabic texts and compiled others. Their work was called
the Cluniac corpus and includes Peter the Venerable's own
synthesis. Although the works were widely distributed,
they were not used to their fullest. Only those sections
that could be most directly and immediately employed in
defense of the Church were selected and quoted without
question. The collection never served as a foundation for
a serious, careful study of Islam, largely due to a total lack
of interest in such an enterprise. Because religious polemic
was directed toward imaginary Muslims, easily eliminated
on paper, a serious study of Islam did not appear to be of
use in any real debate of the issues. In fact, it seems more
likely the aim was to give Christians good reasons to reaf-
firm their own faith. Moreover, unlike the Muslim East,
the Latin West had never focused on religious systems in
and of themselves.[19]

Philosophy was another area where several currents of
interest merged creating a wildly different image of Islam
from that formed in the religious milieu. At first, philosophy seemed little more than an adjunct of science. The
authorized manuals of the natural sciences needed to be
rounded out by works of what we would call scientific
methodology, that is, works on logic, the cosmos, and man
himself. Scientific encyclopedic writers like Aristotle and
much later the Muslim philosopher Avicenna (Ibn Sīnā, d.
1037) have written equally about philosophy. The Latin
West now sought a more complete knowledge of Aristole's
works. In the twelfth century, the only works by Aristotle
available in the West were his brief treatise, *Categories*
and his *De Interpretatione* in the early Latin translations
of Boethius (480?–524). Now, the remainder of the Aristotelian corpus was gradually becoming accessible to a few
scholars through new renditions from the original Greek.
Gerard of Cremona (ca. 1114-87) traveled to Toledo to

locate Arabic versions of Aristotelian texts and his translations of these works contributed to the treasury of Western philosophy.[20] At about the same time a translation
was begun of Avicenna's great philosophical encyclopedia
the *Kitāb al-shifā'* (Book of the Cure). Around 1180, a
first corpus of Avicenna's philosophical works was finished
and put into circulation in Europe.[21] Its influence was
tremendous and translations of other philosophers quickly
followed.

Avicenna gave the Latin West a model of original synthesis. This system incorporated and transcended the various philosophical factions and conflicts of the late twelfth
century, which originated with Saint Augustine, Dionysius
the Areopagite, and Aristotle. The Aristotelian synthesis,
which was truly a scientific conception of the world, was
enhanced by Avicenna's comprehensive analysis of man
and the world. Moreover, Avicenna's work added the dimension of religious salvation and the acceptance of a creative divinity, both essential to Christian thought. Beyond
this, his work suggested an original way of rethinking the
connections between God, the world, and man by encompassing Aristotle's theories of epistemology. The success
of this work is hardly surprising. The English philosopher
Roger Bacon (ca. 1214–92) in his brief outline of the history of philosophy declared: "Thus philosophy was revived
chiefly by Aristotle in Greek and then chiefly by Avicenna
in Arabic."[22]

Western thinkers began to create an image of the Muslim world as the birthplace of the greatest and most wide-
ranging philosophers. This was completely at odds with
the popular image based on preposterous and offensive
myths that saw the Muslim world as a political edifice
at the mercy of a hostile religion. Reconciling these opposite notions presented a real challenge. In this way,
philosopher-theologians adapted Avicenna's Islamic termi-

nology to Christianity. For example, what Avicenna had said regarding the Muslim imam, Roger Bacon applied to the pope.[23]

In certain ways, to the West, the Saracens were seen as a nation of philosophers. Occasionally, as in the works of Peter Abélard (who died in 1142 and was a friend of Peter the Venerable), "philosopher" seems virtually synonymous with "Muslim."[24] A century later, it was to the Saracens, no less, that Thomas Aquinas addressed his *Summa contra Gentiles*, a treatise intended to prove Christian arguments by the light of reason alone "because certain among the gentiles, like the Muslims and the pagans, do not agree with us on the authority of any Scripture."[25] This work was written about 1261–64 at the command of St. Raymond of Peñafort, "a zealous spreader of the faith among the Saracens" to be used in his missionary campaigns in Spain.[26]

One could escape these apparent contradictions about the Muslim world by assuming that their philosophers opposed the official religion of their own countries. Although both too simplistic and too general, this opinion can be substantiated from accurate accounts. From the Western perspective, the Muslim philosophers seemed to accept certain religious dogmas and doctrines that could benefit the ignorant and barbaric among their people. By exaggerating the gap between reason and faith in Islam, some in the West went even further, claiming that the philosophers secretly ridiculed the Qur'ān and were persecuted by the authorities.[27]

The spread of more objective and subtler information about the political and ideological world confronting the Christian West was not only, and perhaps not at all, the automatic result of the increase in facts about Islam: it was rather the response of a gradual change in Western consciousness. Still, conservative Christian theologians attacked the Western disciples of Avicenna and, later, to an even greater extent, those of Averroës (or Ibn Rushd, the Arab philosopher of Spain, 1126–98). Even more, when they attempted to integrate these foreign "stimula" into syntheses of the type that Étienne Gilson, the twenthieth-century neo-Thomist philosopher, referred to as "Avicennist Augustinism," they still met with opposition. And this was more clearly the case when some even founded "Latin Avicennism" and others "Averroism."[28] This must have led to the perception that similar schisms existed in the Islamic world. Many internal factors in the Western world contributed to a rethinking of traditional clichés and attitudes about the Muslim world.

The Muslims did not interest the West for political, military, religious, and scholarly reasons alone. They also aroused a good deal of curiosity in minds eager for strange tales spiced with the exotic. More detailed and sophisticated information resulted from the increased contacts following the reconquest of Spain, the conquest of Muslim Sicily, and the establishment of Latin states in the East. This did not, however, mark an end to the simplistic attitudes toward Islam as a religion or the widespread fabulous tales that served as popular entertainment. Nevertheless, a great deal was learned, much of it accurate, about the geography of the Muslim world, its climate, its cities, its rule, its flora and fauna, as well as details about its farming and industry. In addition, more information became available about the customs of the Saracens, the Bedouins, and later the Tartars, that is, the Mongols. The Saracens had beards, which they valued greatly: they swore by them, and they were disconsolate without them. The turbans they wore protected them from blows in battle and, as a sign of respect, they crossed their hands on their breasts. They ate while seated on mats and buried their most prestigious citizens with jewels, splendid objects, and even images of Muhammad (?). Their laws of hospitality were sacred, for once a man had shared bread and salt with them, his own safety was guaranteed. They respected the elderly; they loved gaudy colors. They were admired for their wealth in gold, silver, precious stones, and magnificent fabrics as well as the palaces of their sovereigns, decorated with gold, silver, and marble, and refreshing fountains. Multicolored birds brought from all over the East and all sorts of animals were to be seen in their menageries.[29] Under the rule of the Saracens were the nomadic Bedouins, who had no permanent living quarters, were tradesmen as well as cattle herders, and were poor soldiers who avoided combat, waiting to see the outcome of any fight so they might pillage the loser's camp.[30]

A fascination with the Muslim world also motivated the first tentative but serious historical studies. In the twelfth century, Godfrey of Viterbo, secretary to the German emperors, added a well-documented summary of Muhammad's life to his *Chronique universelle*.[31] In the early thirteenth century, Cardinal Rodrigo Ximénez (1170?-1247), archbishop of Toledo, wrote the *Historia Arabum*, which contained the first history of the Arabs composed in the West. Beginning with Muhammad and the first caliphs, it concentrated mainly on the activities of the Arabs in Spain.[32]

Though often neglected, there is yet another factor that stimulated additional knowledge of the Muslim world: the economic impulse, that is, the quest for commercial profit. For a great number of European tradesmen, the Muslim world was an economic sphere of primary importance. Initially, business with the Muslim East was transacted through foreign intermediaries, such as Greeks, and Syrians, or semi-foreigners, the Jews. However, already in the ninth century, a portion of this trade was controlled by the Byzantine-dominated Italian cities of Venice, Naples,

Gaeta, and Amalfi, all of which were slowly growing into independent states. The Scandinavians, whose conversion made them members of the Christian community, also began to play an important rôle as intermediaries in this trade. Eventually other Western Christian nations became part of this commercial network, which included a small number of common practices that brought the two worlds closer. For example, Saracen currency circulated and was copied in the West, and Muslim types of commercial contracts were adopted.[33]

It was the pirates among the Saracens that Western merchants first knew and feared. However, the Italians were soon powerful enough to ward them off, and eventually to initiate their own attacks against them. The Italians did not hesitate to enter Saracen territory, at times indulging in rather questionable activities. In Alexandria, for instance, in 828, the Venetians made off with relics of Saint Mark. More often, however, Italian merchants, provided with passports of safe conduct (*amān*), made direct contacts with their Muslim or Eastern Christian counterparts. At first this meant simple contacts with customs agents and minor civil servants, but with the growing volume of commercial trade and the assertion of Western power, those contacts began to involve officials of increasingly higher rank. This trade soon required inter-governmental relations. It was, in fact, at this level that official contacts were established in the ninth century between the cities of Campania, primarily Amalfi, and the Saracens, despite the threats and offers of the pope and the complaints of Emperor Louis II, for whom Naples had turned into another Palermo or Mahdiyya.[34]

The Amalfitans must have had such relations with Palestine at the beginning of the eleventh century, since they were able to rebuild the Church of Santa Maria de Latina in Jerusalem, which was destroyed by the Fāṭimid

Caliph al-Ḥākim. They were even able to hold an annual fair there on the fourteenth of September where anyone paying two pieces of gold could display his merchandise.[35] Even before the first Crusade, the Amalfitans probably had their own quarter in Antioch. Naturally, these limited contacts grew in significance and number after the Crusades. The Italian trade centers proliferated, as is well known, and they came to play an ever more crucial rôle.

To these European merchants, from their own underdeveloped regions, the Muslim world must have appeared a veritable spring of luxury goods: papyrus, ivory, precious fabrics, spices, and some products already in general use, such as olive oil. It was also a market for European raw materials, such as wood, iron, and other metals, tar, slaves, and furs. Gradually the economic positions were reversed and the West began exporting to the East manufactured products such as fabrics, and to a lesser extent, swords from Scandinavia.[36]

Quite clearly, no matter how steadfast they were in their Christian faith, it was impossible for those European merchants who established relations with the Muslim world, to share the commonly held assumptions about the Muslim people themselves. We have occasional but noteworthy evidence of friendly contacts between Western and Eastern merchants.[37] The general impression of these relations put forward by Roberto Lopez, an expert on this subject, is that "the two communities were not on friendly terms but neither did they despise one another as the Greeks and Romans had the barbarians, or the victorious Christians had the pagans." The "unspoken complicity" of the merchants led to feelings of mutual respect.[38]

Respect for the adversary appeared in the totally different area of warfare between Crusaders and Saracens. For all the hostility, the enemy seemed at times to share those values esteemed by the medieval code of chivalry. Recording his immediate impression of the first Crusade, an anonymous Italian knight showed his admiration for the bravery, shrewdness, and military prowess of the Turks in the battle of Dorylaeum in 1097. By his own account, there was mutual respect and he pointed out that the Turks themselves maintain: "they are of the Frankish race and claim that no one, apart from themselves and the Franks, could dare call himself a knight." The author was well aware of the boldness of his words, and noted: "I speak the truth and let no one deny it."[39] He allows that if only the Turks had "remained steadfast to the Christian faith" then "in strength, in bravery, and in the science of war, none could match them."[40]

A century later, the arch-enemy, Saladin (the Sultan Ṣalāḥ al-Dīn, 1138–93) inspired overwhelming admiration among Westerners. In battle, he conducted himself in a humane and chivalrous manner but was little repaid by the Crusaders, especially Richard the Lion-Hearted. During the siege of Acre (1189-91) when cease-fires occurred, soldiers were seen socializing, dancing, singing, and playing with their adversaries. There were even some European women who came to comfort the Crusaders and ended up sharing their favors with Muslims as well.[41] It was in this atmosphere of mutual respect that stories about Saladin first took hold. And, after a period during which the Ayyūbid sultan was represented in an unfavorable light (doubtless because of tales begun among the Levantine Christians, for they displayed a good knowledge of conditions in the area), these new tales praised the glories of Saladin far and wide. In fourteenth-century Flanders a long epic poem was composed about Saladin representing an accumulation of all the legends surrounding him.

Stories were told about how Saladin, dressed up as a donkey (!), had taken Cairo, and had behaved like a true knight. It was said that he traveled to France via Rome, where he was unfavorably impressed by the confessions made to the pope by the French knights who accompanied him. While in Paris, he saw the court give food to twelve paupers in honor of the apostles, but he also noticed how much care was taken to make sure the food was nothing more than scraps.[42] The queen of France, who was one of the wives of Philip II (1180–1223), is said to have fallen in love with Saladin. Their love affair was pursued under the guise of theological discussions. Surely such a perfect knight could not be excluded from the Christian experience. Therefore, his mother was said to be a countess of Ponthieu who had been shipwrecked in Egypt by a storm; and it was recounted that Saladin himself had been converted on his death-bed.[43] Saladin was also credited with seducing Eleanor of Aquitaine (1122–1204), who had gone to Palestine some twenty years before his reign! [44] His name was given to many children and, as a result, is still found as a surname among our contemporaries.

Similarly, the great twelfth-century Muslims, 'Imād-al-Dīn Zangī and Qiliç Arslan (Seljuk atabegs of Mosul and Rūm respectively) were supposed to be of Christian descent, just as at a later date, Thomas à Becket was said to have had a Saracen mother.[45] Moreover, in reality, matrimony had occasionally been planned between European and Muslim rulers.[46]

Toward a Less Polemical Image

A number of factors contributed to the change in the way the West perceived this strange Eastern world: the increase in factual information about Islam and the Muslim world, the steady growth of actual contacts through both political and commercial relations, and even the mutual respect that was the occasional result of these experiences,

the great appreciation for scientific and philosophical principles deeply rooted in the East, and the gradual evolution
within Western consciousness itself. But the key element
in this evolution was the transformation within the Western Christian world itself. Christianity had succeeded as a
viable ideology in part by adopting the Roman administrative model, producing in this way a society under two centers of control: the ideological and the political.[47] While
ideological unity was maintained (in the Latin branch of
Christianity), there was a breakdown in political harmony,
although this was temporarily checked by Charlemagne in
the early ninth century.

The Council of Clermont's decision to embark on the
First Crusade to the Holy Land in 1095 was tied to the
movement toward papal supremacy. These communal expeditions re-established a certain unity, but lacked a single,
independent political center. The influence of centrifugal
political factors was again felt even in the area of Eastern
campaigns, which were ostensibly united under a single
ideology. Monarchies, as they developed, provided a framework for feelings of nationalism, which became more and
more evident throughout Europe. Internal strife, however,
continued to spread, thereby ruining any hope for ideological unity. The only area to experience such unity, and very
slowly at that, was the purely spiritual realm.

When an ideological movement under a unified political command (e.g., modern eastern Europe and China) is
torn by internal dissension, the conflict with any opposing
ideology gradually appears less important than the struggles between members of the same faith. This is especially
true when an ideological element that is at first ancillary—
in both cases proto-national or national consciousness—
begins to reinforce these differences within the faith.

From such a ruthless, polemical image and from the
Manichean "diabolization" of a political and ideological

adversary, there was a smooth transition to more subtle perceptions, at least in some quarters. The image fixed in Western minds during the high Middle Ages and propagated by popular literature continued to influence the general uneducated public. Except for a few cases, there was, as yet, no notion of relative ideology. One such exception was Emperor Frederick II of Hohenstaufen (1194–1250), an Islamophile and Arabist, who could converse about philosophy, logic, medicine, and mathematics in Arabic with Muslims. Indeed, the emperor was strongly influenced by Muslim ways and he set up a colony of Saracens in his service at Lucera in Italy complete with a mosque and all the amenities of the East.[48] Details of Frederick's history are known: his excommunication, his incredible "crusade," his dealings with the Ayyubid sultan of Egypt al-Malik al-Kāmil (1218–38), his friendship with Emir Fakhr al-Dīn ibn al-Shaykh, as well as the pact of 1229 whereby al-Kāmil restored to the Frankish Kingdom various territories, first among them the holy cities of Jerusalem, Bethlehem, and Nazareth. However, even after this restoration, Muslims were still permitted to worship at the Qubbat al-Ṣakhra (the Dome of the Rock), the mosque built above the site of the ancient Temple of Solomon and Herod.[49]

Pope Gregory IX excommunicated Frederick II in 1239. Among other transgressions, the pope accused the emperor of looking favorably on Islam, and maintaining that the world had been deceived by three impostors: Moses, Jesus, and Muhammad. While such a charge may háve been false, as Frederick claimed, it does prove that this notion, which seems to have had its origins in the Muslim world, was also widespread at the time in Christian Europe. Moreover, not long before Frederick II's time, a cleric in Tournai was accused of pronouncing the same blasphemy.[50]

On various occasions, the Muslims were represented
to Christians as paragons of piety, perhaps through the
craftiness of moralists or as part of the well-known wave
of medieval anti-clericalism. However it came about, the
result was to reinforce the tendency to see in the Muslims
the same qualities as in all men: they too worshiped God
in their own way, even if in doing so they were totally in
error.[51]

The best illustration of this attitude from Frederick
II's era can be seen in the work of the Bavarian min-
nesinger, Wolfram von Eschenbach (1170–1220?). Some
of his *Willehalm* is taken directly from the early twelfth-
century French chanson de geste about the siege of Orange (*La Prise d'Orange*). But when Wolfram describes
the fighting between the Saracens and Franks, he ascribes
chivalric virtues to both sides equally and demonstrates a
genuine effort toward understanding the enemy. In Wolfram's tale, the Muslim beauty, Arabele (Orable), is made
a Christian named Gyburg (Guibourg), who appeals for
tolerance. In the words of the poet: "Is it not a sin to
slaughter people who have never heard of Christianity as
we slaughter cattle? I would even say that it is a great
sin, for all men who speak the seventy-two languages are
the creatures of God." Wolfram's *Parzival* similarly bor-
rows from and transforms the *Perceval le Gallois* of his
predecessor, the twelfth-century French poet Chrétien de
Troyes. Here we see Parzival's father, Gahmuret, leaving
for the East, although by no means in the rôle of a Crusader. Quite the contrary, he enlists in the service of the
"baruc" (*mubārak* or "blessed one"?) of Baghdad (Baldag)
who was, as Wolfram knew, the spiritual leader, the Muslim pope. As Wolfram says: "he was given life in Anjou;
he lost it for the baruc at Baghdad."[52] His interment was
at Baghdad, then the capital of the Islamic world. The
baruc provided him a splendid tomb where he was revered

and mourned by the Saracens. As a result of Gahmuret's amatory triumphs, the Saracen knight Feirefitz becomes Parzival's half-brother.

Speculation abounds, some of it quite bold, as to Wolfram's Eastern sources. Regardless of the provenance of these sources, it should be noted that Wolfram renders Arabic names of the planets fairly correctly.[53] He claims that his primary source is a Muslim manuscript discovered at Toledo by the mysterious Kyôt. He also maintains that the work goes back to the magician and astrologer Flegetanis (al-Falak al-Thāni, "The Second Heavenly Sphere"?) who was himself half-Jewish, half-Muslim.[54] It is striking to note that despite its well-known Celtic sources, the *Parzival*—the most honored of all versions of the Grail legend and one of the high points of medieval Christian expression—is an epic replete with Muslim elements and permeated with gnostic and Manichean influences drawn from the Eastern world. Wolfram, apparently a good Christian, nevertheless appeals for an end to the hatred toward pagans (Muslims) who are as they are only because they have not yet heard Christ's message.[55]

The realization of the danger posed by the Mongols, the discovery of a pagan world beyond Islam, and the unleashing of ideological divisions within the Christian world, led to a more tolerant view of Islam. Internal divisions in the West affected the univeralist ideology of Christianity itself. It was no longer merely a question of conflicts between political entities, where there was as yet no significant display of ethnic, proto-national, or national pride.

The Mongol invasions of the thirteenth century were viewed in part according to the earlier polemical view. Many saw these invasions as nothing more than powerful attacks against the Muslim world aimed at the final and long-awaited fall of Islam. The truth was often stretched considerably, whether concerning the strength of Nestori-

anism in Central Asia, the support of some Mongol leaders
for Christianity, or the rôle of certain Christians in the military and state bureaucracy of the Mongol empire. Many
of these false notions can be traced back to the legend
of Prester John, the fabled Christian priest and monarch
of the twelfth century who was believed to have ruled a
great empire in either Africa or Asia. The account of diplomatic contacts whose goal was the formation of a Latin-
Mongol military alliance against the Muslim world is also
on record.

It soon became clear the Mongols were not Christians
and would not necessarily promote the Christian cause.
Indeed, it would be far from easy to win and maintain
their support. They had cruelly enslaved Christian nations and "it is their object to overthrow the whole world
and reduce it to slavery," warned Jean de Plano Carpini
after his diplomatic mission of 1245–47 to the court of
the Mongol khan. He was convinced that if the Mongols
were victorious, they would destroy all of Christianity.[56]
In short, he saw the Mongol danger as much more serious
than any threat from Islam. This immense pagan force,
at once both political and military, singularly complicated
all other problems. The term pagandom could hardly continue to apply solely to Islam. With the accumulated information about central and eastern Asia brought back
by diplomats and merchants, the original division of the
world between Christianity and Islam must have yielded to
a greater flexibility, suggesting a greater relativism in ideological vision. Christians no longer comprised a majority
or even half of the world's population, the remainder being
essentially Muslim. Rather, it had become apparent that
Christians amounted to only one-tenth or perhaps one-
hundredth of humanity in all its variety.[57] The feeling that
Islam shared the same basic concept of religious monotheism with Christianity was reinforced; it was a notion that

recurred earlier only fleetingly. In 1254, under the sponsorship of Louis IX of France, the Franciscan friar, William de Rubruquis, traveled to the Mongol court. There, before the great khan, de Rubruquis participated in a religious disputation in which he took the side of Nestorianism and Islam against Buddhism.[58]

What seemed, as a result of these events, to be a trend toward greater understanding of Islam, was to be short-lived. Roger Bacon and the Catalan ecclesiastic Raymond Lull (ca. 1235?–1316) suggested replacing military operations with missionary work, based on a thorough study of Islamic doctrine and languages. Bacon drew attention to the positive contribution of Islam in the divine plan of revelation. (This position has been taken up again by the more progressive Catholics in their recent ecumenical efforts.[59]) Of course, Islam was still the enemy, but a greater understanding could only result in a more objective view and eventually to a greater relativism. It was at the beginning of the fourteenth century that Dante exempted Avicenna, Averroës, and Saladin from hell and assigned them instead to limbo. Among medieval souls, only they were allowed a reprieve shared by the sages and heroes of antiquity.[60]

In 1312, the Council of Vienne approved the ideas of Bacon and Lull on the learning of languages, notably Arabic. But it was too late. The fall of Acre in 1291 definitively ended all the hopes of the Crusades. It had been some time since the war against the Eastern infidels had been able to unite the West in a common struggle. The plan for the expansion of a united Christian Europe gave way, once and for all, to nationalistic political projects. Only the Reconquista in Spain still continued, and even then along more nationalistic lines. Moreover, since the middle of the thirteenth century, the Muslim states were hardly a danger. Policies related to the Muslim world were given less attention than other matters. The relative tolerance extended to Muslim (and Jewish) subjects of Christian states was a phenomenon practiced only in Spain, and was so peculiar that it could not be maintained for long.

Latin Europe began to focus on its own internal battles, as well as its cultural development, and no longer accorded Islam primary importance in its ideological struggle. By now, Islam was simply no longer of interest to Europe. What really mattered now were the internal ideological problems. To the English theologian John Wycliffe (ca. 1320?–84), it was the reform of the Church that was most important: a return to the purity of pristine Christianity would be sufficient to bring about the decline of Islam. Moreover, the vices for which Islam was blamed were no less common in Latin Christendom. In fact, the Church might as well have been Muslim. Greeks, Jews, and Muslims were no farther from salvation than many Latin Christians.[61] This opinion became as widespread as the "bon mot" about the three impostors (i.e., Jesus, Moses, and Muhammad).[62]

When the great Muslim authors were first discovered, they were something different and innovative. From an intellectual perspective, however, these same writers were now on their way to being subsumed by the common European culture. The works of Avicenna, Averroës, and Algazel in philosophy; Avicenna, Haly ('Alī ibn al-'Abbas), and Rhazes (along with the Christian Arab physician Ibn Māsawayh, called Mesuë) in medicine; and writers in other sciences would be copied, printed, annotated, and studied for centuries to come. Geoffrey Chaucer (d. 1400, who also compiled a *Treatise on the Astrolabe* from the Latin translation of the Arab, Māshā' Allāh) must have encountered a very typical physician in the Tabard Inn at Southwark before beginning the pilgrimage to Canterbury in 1390. This man had little understanding of the Bible but:

Wel knew he the olde Esculapius,
And Deyscorides, and eek Rufus
Olde Ypocras, Haly and Galyen,
Serapion, Razis and Avycen,
Averrois, Damascien and Constantyn,
Bernard, and Gatesden, and
Gilbertyn.[63]

The Arabs may have started out on an equal footing with other "classical" authors, but by the Renaissance, the Greeks were considered the undisputed masters. The earlier translations of classical Greek authors via Arabic were seen as the epitome of the distortion of antiquity by the medieval "gothic" spirit. With the Renaissance came the novel idea of returning to the original texts. The term "Arabism" began to assume negative connotations.[64] Disdain for the barbarian age now included all that was Arab. Petrarch (1304–74) vehemently attacked the style of the Arab poets, although he was almost certainly ignorant of their work.[65]

In no way did this hinder the steady proliferation of cultural borrowings from the Muslim East. Literary borrowing increased, no doubt, because commercial relations were now becoming more common and concentrated. But on the theoretical level, what began as a preoccupation with knowing and understanding Muslim ideology was, in some quarters, turning to complete indifference.

Coexistence and Reconciliation: The Enemy becomes a Partner

As the Ottoman Empire advanced into Christian Europe (namely, the Balkans), concerns about the Muslim religion were briefly rekindled among Western theologians. However, as the Christian concept itself was in a state of decay, it was difficult to revive the spirit of the Crusades. Some theologians began to seriously question whether military effort was truly effective or even useful in its usual form, whether peaceful missionary efforts alone were sufficient, and whether a reconciliation could not be effected between two groups whose religious message was so similar. In the words of R. W. Southern, this was the "moment of vision" between 1450 and 1460 and significantly, also the time of the fall of Constantinople.[66]

In 1454, John of Segovia (ca. 1400–1458) suggested a series of conferences with the *fuqahā'*, or Muslim jurists. Such conferences would be valuable, he believed, even if they did not result in the conversion of the parties involved. Moreover, he did his own translation (no longer extant) of the Qur'ān, which corrected the error of the Cluniac translations, namely, of distorting the original meaning by adapting it to Latin concepts. For his efforts, he met with the displeasure of Jean Germain (ca. 1400–1461), the conservative bishop of Chalon-sur-Saône, who favored military action and the renewal of the spirit of the Crusades. John did, however, win the support of the philosopher and ecclesiastic Nicholas of Cusa (1401–64), who sought practical applications of these proposals. It was Nicholas of Cusa who attempted an accurate philological and historical study of the Qur'ān in his *Cribratio Alchoran* (1460). John of Segovia's efforts also partly inspired a letter in 1460 from Pius II to the Ottoman sultan Mehmed II. The letter, undertaken as an attempt at intellectual persuasion, was a masterpiece of sophisticated dialectic. Still, it was the work of a politician and, as such, was essentially lacking in any genuine sincerity.[67]

The Ottoman Turks were a serious danger, but in the new atmosphere of the fifteenth century, they were seen more as a secular or cultural menace than an ideological threat. The very defenders of the Christian faith were often inspired more by chivalric honor than religious fervor. Many, undoubtedly, still held to the dream of another

crusade and a reconquest of Muslim territories. Of espe-
cial concern were those lands recently usurped from the
Christians, such as the Balkans, where it was confidently
assumed that help would come from a general insurrec-
tion against the Turks.[68] However, the situation at hand
called for more defensive measures. At this stage, European rulers did not consider Christian expansionism worth
the sacrifice of their own political (and eventually national)
interests; nor did the general public see this as justification
for a call to arms throughout Europe, as earlier had been
the case with the Crusaders. Henry VIII made all this quite
clear to the Venetian ambassador in 1516.[69] From then on,
to the realists, the Ottoman Empire became a power like
any other and even a European power. Still, it had been a
long time since any other Muslim power had penetrated
this far into Europe and therefore political relations with
the Ottomans now became essential. Whether it was to
be an alliance, neutrality, or outright war would depend
on political factors quite separate from religion. It was
thought that as long as religion was sufficiently embedded
in the hearts of the faithful, religious considerations could
temporarily be suspended for "serious" political undertak-
ings.

Ottoman emissaries were now beginning to spend more
and more time in European cities such as Venice. Treaties
were even negotiated with the Turks. It was at this time
that Charles VIII of France had illusions of conquering
Italy and establishing a base there to recapture Constantinople and Jerusalem. Meanwhile, between 1490 and
1494, the Ottoman sultan, Bāyezīd II, was making an annual payment to the papacy for the continued imprisonment in Italy of his brother and rival, Djem. In 1493,
Bāyezīd's ambassador in Rome participated in a secret
consistory presided over by the Borgia Pope Alexander
VI, which included cardinals, bishops, and European en-

voys. Here the sultan's representative was received with the greatest reverence and ceremony. In his *Mémoires*, the chronicler Philippe de Commynes (1447?–1511) writes the following quite unthinkable words for a medieval mind: "The Turk ... straightaway dispatched an emissary to the Venetians ... who, upon orders of the pope, severely warned them [the Venetians] to take up arms against the king of France [Charles VIII]."[70] The pope actually sent the sultan a letter (for which we still have the text) that denounced Charles VIII's plans for a crusade and demanded that the sultan secure Venetian intervention against the French. The pope warned Bāyezīd to hold back "for a while" from attacking Hungary or other Christian countries, actions that would put the papacy in an embarrassing situation. In return, the Ottoman sultan recommended elevating Nicholas Cibo to the cardinalate, and above all else, executing Djem on condition of a payment of 300,000 ducats; he also took an oath on the Qur'ān not to harm any Christians.[71] Apparently both sides met with agreement.[72]

In 1497, Milan, Ferrara, Mantua, and Florence conspired to finance an Ottoman attack on Venice.[73] Two years later, as Venice and France were on the verge of attacking Milan, Ludovico il Moro, the Duke of Milan, and other Italian princes told Bāyezīd in no uncertain terms that if Milan were captured, a crusade would soon follow. The sultan responded by declaring war on Venice.[74] Several decades later when Suleymān the Magnificent was conquering Hungary and virtually turning the Mediterranean into an Ottoman lake, Francis I entered into an active alliance with him and they combined their military forces against Charles V in 1535. However, the French monarch still felt the need to rely on Christian doctrine and ideology as a justification for this alliance. But by the late sixteenth century, religious arguments completely gave way to political realities. In 1588, Elizabeth I even went so far as to inform Sultan Murād III that, as far as she was concerned, Spain was nothing but a nation of idolaters with Philip II as their leader. An alliance based solely on ideology was now proposed: strict monotheists against untrustworthy Catholics.[75] That such an alliance could have been proposed is noteworthy, even given Elizabeth's insincerity. Such political deals as those described were not uncommon at the time of the Crusader states but these came under the heading of colonial policy. It was quite a different matter when such things occurred in the heart of Europe. In Italy, not only had every state of any importance sought, at one time or another, the assistance of the Turks in fending off their rivals, but entire regions let their oppressive governments know that they would gladly welcome an eventual Turkish invasion, just as some Balkan Christians had.[76]

While the Ottoman Turks may therefore have been accepted as Europeans of a sort, they were hardly integrated into every aspect of the European experience. Clearly, ideological contention, religious hostilities, were still very much present. According to Norman Daniel, the West's image of Islam fashioned in the Middle Ages was both polemical and apologetic.[77] It was an attitude that was, for the most part, contemptuous and uncomprehending, and it continued basically unchanged. Still, Islam seemed a less unusual and offensive issue considering the degree of religious hatreds within the Christian community itself. In the Middle Ages, Islam had been considered a schism, a kind of perversion of Christianity. This was, for example, how Dante regarded it. It was a time of an increasing number of schisms within the Church, expressed not only by religious differences but by political ambitions as well. This was the case with Islam, and indeed, it could now be seen as a mere schism, one of many such, and necessarily the most dangerous.[78]

On the cultural level as well, the Turks were being brought into the ethnic fold of the European nations by bogus genealogies then in vogue. Thus, the Turks, just like the French and the Italians, were seen as the descendants of the Trojans, of the Trojan King Priam, or of his ancestors. Others could not accept such arguments, which legitimized Ottoman rule in Anatolia and revolved around the notion that the Ottoman conquests of Greece and the Balkans were, in all events, an exaggerated retribution against the ancient deeds of Agamemnon and his followers. Instead, these people preferred to believe the Turks were descendants of the Scythians, which in turn gave rise to the humanist version of the age-old Christian hostility toward the Muslims.[79] At issue now was not so much a campaign against infidels as a defense against barbarians (*bellum contra barbaros*, as it was often characterized at the time): to those Europeans brought up on Herodotus and Xenophon, this was an enticing notion.

The Turks were now virtually undifferentiated from Islam itself; indeed, the word "Turk" was becoming a synonym for "Muslim." There was also a growing awareness of the Persians and their political and religious enmity toward the Ottoman Empire, which offered possibilities for intricate political stratagems. Contacts were established in even more remote areas, for example with the Muslims of India and their magnificent rulers, the great Mughals. As for the Arabs, they had been reduced to a political nonentity, and appeared to be of very minor importance in the West's perception of the Middle East. They were seen as little more than pillaging Bedouins, a stereotype that had remained unchanged since at least the time of Joinville. The term "Saracen" gradually disappeared from common usage.

Regardless of whether or not the Muslim Turks were descended from Sycthian barbarians, as some pedants argued, they nevertheless remained the masters of the most powerful empire in Europe. Constantinople was theirs, and this city of marvels was made even more accessible by improved communication. The majesty of the Sublime Porte made a lasting impression on the Europeans; the force of its presence overpowered them. Louis XIV risked excommunication by sending soldiers to Rome in 1687 when the pope dared to ask him to waive the privileges of his embassy, which had been gradually extended to include an entire district of the city and was a haven for all kinds of scoundrels. But, he allowed his ambassadors at Constantinople to suffer imprisonment, humiliation, and taxation, and their staffs to be subjected to unending tribulation.[80]

From Coexistence to Objectivity

The West began to move toward a more objective undertanding of the Middle East because of a number of changing factors: geographical proximity, close political relations, increasing economic interactions, the growing number of travelers and missionaries who journeyed to the East, and the passing of a unified Christianity in Europe. For politicians and merchants, an unbiased appraisal of the East was becoming an ever more pressing necessity. Descriptions that were detailed, precise, and as far as possible, objective were more numerous after the publication of the Middle East pilgrimage of Arnold von Harff in 1496.[81] A greater objectivity was brought to the study of Muslim values: Muslim practices were no longer seen simply as the opposite of traditional Christian morality. There were even inquiries into the political, administrative, and military systems of the Ottoman Empire. These studies, while frequently critical, now also recognized the Ottoman achievements in many areas.[82] Europeans saw the Muslim East as a land of wealth and prosperity: an advanced civilization of grand monuments and sumptuous courts of unimagined splendor.

The Renaissance's cosmopolitanism and encyclopedism, with the mannerisms of its cultural expression, had allowed the Muslim East and Near Eastern studies their due. However, curiosity about the East had not yet turned into exoticism, that is, the thrill of "escape," that sense of being transported through art or lifestyle without ever leaving one's own culture. The first hints of any real exoticism were linked to isolated cases, for example, those travelers who, after returning from the East, began to dress like Turks.[83] But, the Eastern world was more often given a Western guise than the reverse. Underlying Western conceptions were clear even when works were heightened by magic and marvels as in the works of the Italian poets, Ariosto (1474–1533) and Tasso (1544–85), even when some episodes or themes were geniunely of Eastern origins, and even when the subject matter was drawn entirely from Eastern history as in Marlowe's *Tamburlaine*.[84] But while these works of pure fantasy may have thrilled the literary public, no one took them seriously as a source of information about the history or character of the Muslim East.

Gradually, however, first-hand accounts brought back by travelers and diplomats began to reach an ever-widening audience. In the arts, there was a growing fascination with the idea of local color. For example, in paintings of the life of Jesus or the martyrs, whenever the men of the Sanhedrin or Oriental potentates were portrayed, they were always shown wearing the stereotypical turban. And, from his "Moorish" roots, Othello kept only one item: the fatal magic handkerchief that an Egyptian sorceress had given his mother.[85] Molière went even further: he took the trouble to include actual Turkish phrases as part of the Oriental scene in *Le Bourgeois Gentilhomme* (1670). In 1672, in the preface to his tragedy, *Bajazet*, Jean Racine (1639–99), stressed the care he had taken to educate himself in Turkish history. Even so, Pierre Corneille (1606–84) and others criticized Racine for not having created in his play a single character "who has the feelings that he ought to have, that people at Constantinople have. Though wearing Turkish dress, they all express the feelings common in France."[86] In later prefaces to the play, Racine responded to his critics: "I have sought in this tragedy to faithfully depict what is known to us of the manners and maxims of the Turks."

From the Middle Ages on, literature had continually embraced exotic subjects. Indeed, many authors supported efforts to enhance literary works with correct information about the Middle East. Exoticism broke into art in the seventeenth century and swamped it in the eighteenth. Even accurate data about Eastern civilizations, eventually incorporated into Western art and literature, became distorted. This was an inevitable consequence of being integrated into an altogether different world vision, which it considered truly universal. Still, it took a long time to advance from the abstract notion of the relativity of civilizations, which was clearly formulated in the eighteenth century, to the integration of exotic facts into wholes that were free of all ethnocentricism. This process, it is fair to note, has not even been achieved in our time.

Assimilating the exotic began with the erosion of the privileged position of Christianity in European civilization. Christianity began to give way to new ideologies, and with the latter came new sensibilites and tastes, though even these were European and privileged. But, objective study of the Muslim world became possible the moment Islamic values and ideas were no longer considered completely in error. Political realities and the impartial observations of travelers and merchants helped pave the way. To this was added the new focus on erudition.

Scholarly research tends to be relatively objective even when it is at the service of a militant ideology within a greater social context, all the more so if its militant designs begin to blur and to wither away. Half-truths were used to bolster a particular position yet they tended to become even more distorted in the process. The purpose of scholarship is to strive after truth for its own sake. But facts, in an almost unconscious way, are still integrated into more or less slanted synthetic conceptions. Nevertheless, real progress has already been made when there is no longer a prior and willful selection, manipulation, or embellishment of these facts to suit a conscious ideological synthesis.

The Birth of Orientalism

At first the study of Eastern languages and the compiling of related material was motivated by ideology alone. Already in medieval Spain, Arabic studies had been initiated to serve the needs of the missionary cause. Interest in these studies faded when Granada fell in 1492 leaving only a small group of Moriscos who spoke a Romance language instead of Arabic. Eastern studies were taken up instead in Rome where they were integrated into the curriculum of Semitic studies as the curia attempted to bring the Eastern churches under Vatican control. Political and commercial concerns as well as the new humanist interest in a more universal culture helped consolidate these earlier efforts into a body of Muslim studies. Guillaume Postel (1510–81), a thoroughly committed scholar in spite of his mysticism, his zealous devotion to the service of the faith, his French patriotism, and even his insanity, contributed enormously to the study of languages, and peoples, while assembling an important collection of manuscripts in the East.[87] Postel's student, Joseph Scaliger (1540–1609), a man of encyclopedic learning, even abandoned his earlier Christian work to explore Orientalism.

Because of the capabilites of the printing works established by the Medici Cardinal Ferdinand Grand Duke of Tuscany, by 1586 it became possible to print works in Arabic for the first time. Of course, the ostensible purpose for establishing these printing facilities was to further the missionary effort. But from the beginning, everything was published, from Avicenna's medical and philosophical works to books of grammar, geography, and mathematics. There were similar publishing ventures at the end of the sixteenth and the beginning of the seventeenth centuries in Paris, Holland, and Germany, often aimed at a better understanding of Avicennan medicine.

This period saw a new flowering of science and erudition serving various political, ideological, and economic interests that financed and supported this scholarship. Economic growth, under the control and protection of powerful states, made a more advanced knowledge not only desirable, but often necessary. The relatively organized nature of patronage at high levels encouraged a certain degree of specialization, which contrasted sharply with the individualistic encyclopedism of the Renaissance. Out of these efforts, an organized network was developed, patronized, and financed by states for the acquisition and dissemination of information. At the same time, the idea originated that the pursuit of scientific knowledge was a civic duty.[88] Specialization and a certain amount of organization required cooperation among the increasing number of researchers. As a result, individual dreams and ambitions narrowed considerably, while there arose what could be called a "regional objectivity." A specialist could focus on one topic within certain limitations and go on to analyze it conscientiously. Relieved of any synthetic concerns, he could ignore the ideological, philosophical, political, or social interpretations, which others might draw from his work. From the seventeenth century on, there were few anxious to reach such conclusions in the tradition of the Renaissance encyclopedists. And these few were regarded as more or less eccentric dreamers, in a completely different world from the "serious scholars." Alone with these dreamers were the philosophers. The human sciences had not yet developed to a point where they could be considered on their own terms or as more than an adjunct to general philosophy. Objectivity was also favored by the new ideological pluralism in Europe following the end of the religious wars (which had resulted in a virtual stalemate) and by the growing cooperation among scientists now allied to different ideologies.

These general factors also influenced the whole area of Orientalism. The papacy and many Christians sought to unite the Eastern and Western churches by studying their languages and texts. However, trade and political designs in the East were the major concerns of England, France, and the United Provinces. As travel became easier, Maronite scholars found their way to Europe and in 1611, at Conflans, the Dutch Orientalist, Thomas van Erpe (Erpenius; 1584–1624) even encountered a Muslim merchant from Morocco. Biblical exegesis, a subject of the first rank in discussions between Protestants and Catholics, also contributed to an appreciation of Eastern philology. Moreover, for all the lingering "anti-Arabist" sentiment, Avicenna's work still continued to command the respect of physicians. Both the Ottoman Empire and Islam itself came under closer scrutiny as a result of the Turkish threat. However, as the empire itself became less of an actual danger, such inquiries could be pursued in a more relaxed atmosphere. Eastern courts were now obliged to recognized Europe's growing political and cultural dominance and as a result, began to take notice of those practical skills the ever-increasing European travelers brought with them to the East, most notably advances in the military arts.

Concerns created by closer links and historical circumstances set the stage for the birth of a closely knit Orientalist network. The first Arabic chair was created in Paris in 1539 for Guillaume Postel at the new Collège de France. He was, as already noted, the epitome of the visionary Renaissance scholar: not only was he responsible for some of the first handbooks published, but most notably, he prepared students such as Joseph Scaliger, who was already a fairly strong Orientalist himself. There were now manuscript collections in the libraries and their availability enabled scholars to establish a serious education for themselves. With advances in printing—especially the recent developments in printing Arabic script—scholars could now gain much greater access to each other's work. One after another, intellectual specialists set out to produce their own indispensable tools of scholarship: grammars, dictionaries, texts. Among the most prominent in this effort were two Dutchmen: Jacob Golius (1596–1667) and his teacher Thomas van Erpe, who published the first Arabic grammar and the first edition of a text done according to strict philological methods. In 1680 in Austria, Franz Meninski of Lorraine published his exhaustive Turkish dictionary. Oriental studies spread beyond Paris, once the lone center in the field, and numerous chairs were now established throughout Europe. Frans van Ravelingen (or Raphelengien [Latinized, Raphelengius], 1539–97) taught Arabic at Leiden as early as 1593. In 1627, Urban VIII founded the College of Propaganda in Rome, which was a bustling center of Oriental studies. And in 1638, Edward Pococke (1604–91) inaugurated an Arabic chair at Oxford.

Aspiring to scientific methodology with ascetic devotion, these scholars amassed research tools, materials, and studies, which at times conflicted with the dominant European ideology and perception of things, though no conscious effort was made to alter this image or to seriously question its validity. In fact, more often than not, the Orientalists were conformists. But, on the other hand, they were influenced by the general climate of the late seventeenth and eighteenth centuries: that is, at least they were no longer required to assume certain apologetic or polemical positions in their work. Sufficient evidence of their loyalty to Christianity was provided by declarations of personal belief (whether sincere or not), which were superimposed on their work without affecting its fundamentally neutral content.[89]

Ideological relativism influenced the thinking of intellectuals and the enlightened public before it reached the Orientalist scholar.[90] Still, the atmosphere thus created had a liberating effect on scholarly research. Those drawn to the Muslim East by a deeply felt personal predilection could continue their research freely. From an already abundant supply of material, the French Orientalist, Barthélemy d'Herbelot (1625–95) compiled his *Bibliothèque Orientale* (published posthumously by Galland in 1697), which could be regarded as the first version of the *Encyclopedia of Islam*. Antoine Galland (1646–1715) made a monumental contribution to the growing mystique of the Orient when he published his translation of the *Arabian Nights* between 1704 and 1717: its influence was to be incalculably great.[91] Thereafter, the Muslim world no longer appeared the province of the Antichrist, but rather as an essentially exotic, picturesque world where fantastic genies could, at their whim, do good or evil. For a public that had already shown a decided taste for European fairy tales, all of this was pure enchantment.[92]

The Enlightenment

In the beginning, there were purely practical courses that were followed outside Christian ideology. Around these, broad outlines of localized or "regional ideologies" began to crystallize. As these ideologies gradually developed ever more daringly into more complete systems, they began to assert not only an independence from Christianity but even an opposition to it. The worldview remained monolithic, but the authoritarianism of Christianity was replaced by the rationalist, progressive, and secular philosophy of the Enlightment. The struggle now was against the medieval concept of the world, a view still supported and defended by the established political powers. Moreover, the argument against "medieval obscurantism," which had continued since the Renaissance, hereafter became a battle against Christianity itself, which seemed unable to disassociate itself from the ideology built during the Middle Ages around its main original themes. Indeed, Christianity, particularly in Catholic countries, retained its political affiliations, which, in turn provoked increasingly angry opposition from the rising social classes.

While it had at one time competed with Christianity as a religious ideology, Islam could now be considered impartially and even sympathetically. Those who did so were unwittingly looking for (and clearly discovering) in Islam the identical qualities of those new Western ideologies opposed to Christianity. By pointing out the merit and sincerity of Muslim beliefs, many seventeenth-century authors defended Islam against medieval intolerance and polemical disparagement. An example of this was the French theologian Richard Simon (1638–1712). While remaining a devout Catholic, he was also a learned scholar and, as such, he persistently struggled against the distortion of objective data to satisfy dogma whether in Biblical in-

terpretation or the study of Eastern Christianity. In his
*Histoire critique de la créance et des coutumes des na-
tions du Levant* (1684), he considered first the faith and
rites of the Eastern Christians, and then those of the
Muslims, which he described clearly and reasonably. He
based his work, without condemnation or condescension
and occasionally with real appreciation and even admiration, on that of a Muslim theologian. When he came
under attack by the philosopher and Jansenist theologian
Antoine Arnauld (1612–94) for not being more critical of
Islam, Simon advised Arnauld to consider the "excellent
lessons" of the Muslim moralists.[93] In 1705, Adriaan Reland (1676–1718), a Dutch Arabist, whose knowledge of Islam surpassed Simon's, wrote an unprejudiced account of
the Muslim religion drawn entirely from Muslim sources.[94]
The French philosopher Pierre Bayle (1647–1706), an ad-
mirer of Muslim tolerance, included in his *Dictionnaire
historique et critique* (first edition, 1697) an objective biography of Muhammad, which was revised according to
new scholarship in later editions.

For the following generation of scholars, the move was
from objectivity to admiration. As an example to Christians, Bayle and many other writers drew attention to
the Ottoman Empire's tolerance toward all sorts of religious minorities. This was the period when (following
the lead established by the Spanish Jews after the In-
quisition of 1492) the Calvinists of Hungary and Transylvania, the Protestants of Silesia, and the Cossack Old
Believers of Russia found refuge in Turkey or turned to
the Porte as they sought to escape Catholic or Orthodox
persecution.[95] Islam was seen as a rational religion, quite
remote from those Christian tenets that most opposed reason. Moreover, Islam seemed to espouse few mythical concepts and mystical traditions, only what was deemed necessary to assure the following of the people. Beyond that,

Islam appeared to balance the demand for a moral life with an understandable respect for the needs of the flesh, the senses, and social interaction. It was, all told, a religion that approximated the Deism of most Enlightenment philosophers. Seen historically, the civilizing rôle of Islam became clearer: civilization did not come from the monasteries, but rather from the pagan Greeks and Romans and was transmitted to Europe by, of all people, non-Christian Arabs.[96]

The German philosopher, Gottfried Wilhelm von Leibniz (1646-1716) already shared these ideas. Shortly after Leibniz, a tract with the provocative title *Mahomet no impostor, or a Defence of Mahomet* (1720) was published anonymously.[97] In 1730, the French historian Henri de Boulainviliers (1658–1722) published his apologetic *Vie de Mahomet*. Of course, one of the most notable admirers of Muslim civilization was Voltaire, though even he vacillated between opposing attitudes about the ideological validity of Islam. He could defend Muhammad as a profound political thinker and the founder of a rational religion. But he could also take advantage of the official faith of his country to denounce that same Muhammad as the prototype of all the impostors who used religious fables to enslave souls.[98]

The Enlightenment ultimately won out and influenced even the specialists, especially those who worked outside the academic community. For example, there was the English lawyer and Arabist George Sale (ca. 1697–1736), an enlightened Christian who published a remarkable translation of the Qur'ān in 1734, introduced by a "Preliminary Discourse," and annotated with succinct, restrained, and accurate notes, which were used by many later writers. An incomparable and passionately devoted student of Arabic literature and history was the self-taught German scholar Johann Jakob Reiske (1716–74). For his efforts, this indefatigable genius was persecuted by the Dutch Orientalists

Albert Schultens (1686–1750) and Johann David Michaelis (1717–91), who sought to keep Arabic studies within the confines of "sacred philology" and biblical exegesis as before. Reiske's erudition, however, did not prevent him from acknowledging a quality of the divine in the creation of Islam.[99] The first attempt to make Orientalist research available to the general public was the *History of the Saracens* by the Oxford professor, Simon Ockley (1678–1720). In this work, published between 1708 and 1718, Ockley favored the Muslim East over the Christian West.[100]

Both erudite details and general ideas found their way into important works of the period. For example, some of this information was consolidated into the work of such writers as Voltaire, and the great English historian Edward Gibbon (1737–94), whose balanced appreciation secured an important place for the Muslim world in the cultural and intellectual history of mankind. A myth was developing: that of Muhammad as a sovereign and lawgiver who was tolerant and wise.[101]

The eighteenth century saw the Muslim East through fraternal and understanding eyes. The idea that all men were born with equal abilities, along with the prevailing optimism (the real religion of the age) now made it possible to seriously reconsider the earlier charges leveled against the Muslim world. There was, to be sure, abundant cruelty and barbarity in the East, but was there really no savagery in the West? Among other examples, it was pointed out that slavery, in a country such as Turkey, was less harsh than elsewhere and that there were indeed also pirates among the Christians.[102] Despotism was, of course, abhorrent but it could be studied and explained by geographical and social causes just like any other political system. Although local conditions in the East might well have favored the rise of despotism, such conditions occasionally developed elsewhere as well. Montesquieu (1689–

1755), who firmly believed in a kind of geographical determinism, identified the third Flavian emperor of Rome, Domitian (A. D. 51–96), as the forerunner of the sophy of Persia.[103]

Whereas the rather liberal sexual attitudes of Islam (as least for men) had been shocking (or unconsciously attractive) to medieval sensibilites, these same attitudes were now becoming highly exciting to a society increasingly preoccupied with eroticism. In the Enlightenment, the Muslims were not singled out as being different from other men. In fact, if anything many of them were considered superior to Europeans. "The Turk, where bigotry interferes not with his better feelings, is as charitable as he is confiding," wrote the English antiquarian Thomas Hope (ca. 1770–1831), who lived in the East on various occasions at the end of the eighteenth century.[104] At the conclusion of *Candide*, the heroes arrive at Constantinople where they find peace at last, acting on the advice of both a hard-working, level-headed old Muslim who was unconcerned with politics and a "famous dervish reputed to be the best philosopher among the Turks."

Travelers to Eastern lands were numerous in this period; many of them were narrow-minded, such as the missionaries who lived in the East in their own hermetic worlds. However, a few like the Scottish explorer James Bruce (1730–94), the German explorer Carsten Niebuhr (1733–1815), the English travelers Henry Maundrell (1665–1701), Richard Pococke (1704–65), and Thomas Shaw (1694–1751), and the French scholars and travelers Jean de la Roque (1661–1754) and Claude-Étienne Savary (1750–88), brought back unusual and fascinating details. This information was added to the accounts of Jean Chardin (1643–1713) and Jean Baptiste Tavernier (1605–89), which were constantly in vogue among the reading public. In Constantinople, Lady Mary Wortley Montague (1689–

1762) entered the world of Muslim women and described it without mystery or myth.[105] Some Easterners, mostly Christians, even ventured into Europe. The young Jean-Jacques Rousseau (1712–78) expressed no surprise when he encountered near Neufchâtel a would-be Archimandrite of Jerusalem, who was more than likely just a Greek adventurer and a subject of the Ottoman sultan.[106] Rousseau, himself, had relatives scattered about the Middle East. His father was a clock-maker attached to the imperial palace in Constantinople, and whose relatives included a consul in Persia whose son held consulates in Basra, Aleppo, Baghdad, and Syrian Tripoli. The literary trope of the Turkish spy who sharply criticizes European manners and customs was first employed in 1684 by the Genoese adventurer Giovanni Paolo Marana, a long-time resident of Egypt. This was to inspire many authors for years to come, most notably Montesquieu in his famous *Lettres Persanes* (1721).[107]

Elsewhere, the pre-Romantic trend begun by Antoine Galland, namely the fascination with the exotic, exchanting Muslim East continued to hold the public imagination. It produced masterpieces like William Beckford's "Arabian tale," *Vathek*, published in 1781. In 1788 in Madrid, Beckford even took as a lover a young Muslim named Muhammad. This trend is enlivened by the strong tendency toward esoterism that characterizes the late eighteenth century, the symbol of which is the Italian pseudo-mystic Count Alessandro di Càgliostro (1743–95), who styled himself the Grand Cophta and boasted of his extended journeys in the East.

A somewhat less fantastical aestheticism motivated the English Orientalist William Jones (1746–94) to study Eastern literatures. Still, like Voltaire and so many others, he Westernized the original form and content of that literature: for example, Arabic verse was put into Greek or

Latin meters. However, there were also those who, along with the encyclopedists of the Enlightenment, remained committed to a more realist, positive, and universalist out-look. This spirit produced men like the Comte de Volney (1757–1820), whose *Voyage en Égypte et en Syrie* (1787) is a masterpiece of meticulous research. With the greatest disdain for the picturesque, Volney was utterly committed to objective observation and showed unusual discernment in political and social matters. While he was an impressive scholar, even mastering Eastern languages, it was the con-temporary world that really interested him.[108] He played a major part in the preparations for the Napoleonic expedi-tion into Egypt. This led to the admirable *Description de l'Égypte* (1809–22), a collection of accurate and thorough archaeological, geographical, demographic, medical, tech-nological, and (anticipating the term) sociological studies, which remain unequaled to this day.

Volney knew Eastern history well, but he believed the best way to understand the past was to observe the present. In his efforts to create an interest in the study of spoken Arabic, he was critical of scholars who knew a great deal about medieval Arab grammarians but were incapable of the most basic conversation in modern Arabic.

A passionate preoccupation with the present and for understanding the true mechanics of things was hardly conducive to the study of pure philology, which conse-quently declined throughout the eighteenth century. Ma-ronites, like the Assemanis in Italy and Miguel Casiri (1710–91) in Spain, catalogued collections of manuscripts. Louis XIV in 1700 and Maria Theresa in 1754 estab-lished schools where interpreters could be trained. In 1784, William Jones founded, in India, the first scholarly society for Orientalists, the Asiatic Society of Bengal. In Muslim India there was a group of Britons who were interested in both Muslim and classical Indian languages and literatures. In 1800 the East India Company, also for practical reasons, established Fort William College in Calcutta. There, many Persian and Arabic classics, manuals, and other research tools were translated (often by native writers) and published. A knowledge of the East was still considered a basic necessity in India. However, by about 1820 Western influences began to prevail and expertise in Indian matters was no longer required. In 1835, Lord Macaulay (1800–1859) imposed the British model on the entire Indian school system.[109]

The Nineteenth Century: Exoticism, Imperialism, Specialization

By the beginning of the nineteenth century, three major trends stood out: a sense of Western superiority marked by pragmatism, imperialism, and utter contempt for other civilizations; a romantic exoticism mesmerized by a magical East whose growing poverty seemed only to add to its charm; and a specialized erudition focused on the great ages of the past. For all their apparent differences, these three conditions were actually more interrelated than antithetical.

Romantic exoticism—of which the Oriental mystique was only one variety—did not arise from any change in the contacts between East and West, but rather from a change within Western sensibilities. It was not just a taste for escapism: the emphasis was now on the most singular, the most individual, in the conception and in the picture painted of the foreign. In the past, what was foreign was always understood to be strange as well, but now only the most bizarre scenes satisfied European tastes. This fascination with the exotic began with the Enlightenment. Starting with Rousseau, the trend was toward the primacy of the individual and his feelings as well as a fascination with the wild and rustic qualities of nature. And, with its love

for so-called primitive poetry, English pre-Romanticism
can be traced to this. This same atmosphere surely influenced a mind such as William Jones's and must have
borne upon the German Sturm und Drang movement and
its supporter Herder (1744–1803), with his own interest in
Eastern literatures. Herder's essays in historical synthesis
place the Muslim contribution in the first rank, and to
him, the Arabs had, in fact, been "Europe's teachers."

For a long time, however, the desire to understand exotic worlds was linked to the classical, universalist vision
that hoped to find in the East, as elsewhere, those human
qualities that transcended time and place. The poems of
Goethe that glorified Muhammad and, in particular, his
much-admired *Mahomets Gesang* of 1774 are incompara-
bly more poetical, though still less vivid in local color,
than the *Mahomet* (1742) of Voltaire. More than forty
years later, in 1819, Goethe wrote his *West-östlicher Divan*, which includes twelve *nameh*s (books), as well as an
opening call for an Eastern "hegira" where the poet will
recover his youth at the spring of Khiḍr (Chiser). To all
of this he added scholarly notes and comments steeped
in Oriental erudition. With his usual sense of intellectual
honesty, Goethe apologized for not concealing his European origins: his unmistakable style revealed him as a
foreigner.[110] The German theologian and Orientalist Adal-
bert Merx (1838–1909) may have been too harsh when he
called Goethe's East a "nonexistent phantasmagoria," but,
as Henri Lichtenberger (1864–1941) has pointed out, "he
was not interested in portraying either the East or the
West per se, but rather, man himself, as intuitively he
found him in one as much as in the other."[111]

It was now 1819, and Goethe still held the attitudes
of an earlier generation. Originating in Germany, the reaction against classicism began to reach a fever pitch. This
was in large part due to the new trends of thought rising

from the failure, or the ambiguous triumph, of the French revolution and from the awakening of German nationalism. By 1800, Friedrich Schlegel (1772–1829) could even declare that the gothic and Orientalist movements were united against classicism. "It is to the East," he wrote, "that we must turn to find the ultimate romanticism (*das höchste Romantische*)" and, following his own advice, he began to study Indian civilization.[112] The bourgeois prose of the new age was now surpassed, not by integrating it in the classical way into universal themes, but rather by a magical and unbounded subjectivity and a fascination with the barbaric and the strange.[113]

This attitude certainly contributed to the new popularity of Oriental studies, which seemed a veritable Renaissance.[114] It also provided the Romantics with an abundance of literary material. Nonetheless, Orientalist erudition grew out of the concerns of the Enlightenment. Anyone in Europe who seriously intended even an introductory study of the languages and civilizations of the Near East ended up at the École des langues orientales vivantes in Paris. This school was established by the Convention of March 1795 at the instigation of Louis Mathieu Langlès (1763–1824), an Orientalist of questionable merit. Langlès, who was the school's first administrator, emphasized the more practical, utilitarian side of language study, but only after first stressing the importance of Eastern languages to the "progress of literature and sciences."[115]

The real innovator in this area was paradoxically Silvestre de Sacy (1758–1838), a Legitimist and Jansenist who was devoted to the values of the past. He considered linguistics, for example, within the framework of an abstract universalism as already defined by the *Grammaire générale et raisonnée* (1660) of the Port-Royal Jansenists. Sacy rose to be the foremost European Orientalist, and Paris became the Mecca of those specializing in Near Eastern studies.[116] He was an exacting philologist who was always extremely careful not to draw any simplistic conclusions nor to advance anything unsupported by the texts. As such, he was a kind of early positivist. He imposed on the world of European specialists the rigorous purism toward which his Jansenism predisposed him. Even today, his style of work has remained that of many Orientalists. The criticisms that are now leveled at this attitude were discernible in Sacy's own time. Volney, for example, and later Ernest Renan, complained that such a style could easily lead to a narrow-minded kind of scholarship, though this was hardly an inevitable consequence of Sacy's method. Indeed, there is little evidence of such a fault among Sacy's most gifted followers.

Scholarly asceticism tended to separate the problems of the past from those of the contemporary world, occasionally to the detriment of an understanding of the former. Also, such asceticism often unwittingly assimilated the notions that were common in its own environment. By disallowing superficial conclusions and syntheses, Sacy's technique ran certain risks: it could result in a rather sterile agnosticism or serve as the uncritical conduit of implicit ideologies whose acceptance was then assured because of such impressive scholarship. But this was just the negative aspect of what was a rather remarkable approach to research and an essential aid to scientific progress. The distrust of certain brilliant and facile syntheses may have included unjustified suspicions about valid and important theories, but it was nonetheless a necessary condition for grounding new structures on a solid base.

A further condition was the final severance of all ties with theology, an inevitable consequence of the political climate in both France and England in the eighteenth century. For example the practical matter of training dragomans in Paris and Vienna had led to the liberation of teaching from theological fetters and resulted in the creation of the École des langues orientales.[117] The school, which was both scholarly and secular, grew out of France's revolutionary fervor and, under the devout Sacy, became the model Orientalist institution. In German-speaking countries, however, the universities were still under theological jurisdiction. As a result, secular Orientalism was initially pursued by amateurs, among whom one of the most prominent was the prolific Josef von Hammer-Purgstall (1774–1856). He was a graduate of the Oriental Academy of Vienna and a professional dragoman. He lacked philological precision but was an unequaled popularizer of knowledge about the East. Moreover, he founded the first specialized Orientalist journal in Europe, the *Fundgruben des Orients* (1809–18), which included essays on the past and the present and to which all European Orientalists, as well as some Eastern scholars, contributed.[118]

The trend toward objectivity and arduous specialized work was in line with the deeper currents of an age in which scientific research was being organized in depth, and of a society in which capitalism was inspiring unprecedented industrial development. Throughout Europe, Silvestre de Sacy's teaching was a success, and institutions for specialized research began to flourish. In 1821 the Société Asiatique of Paris was founded and in 1823 it introduced its own publication, the *Journal Asiatique*. The *Journal of the Royal Asiatic Society of Great Britain and Ireland* appeared in 1834; the society itself was founded in 1823. In 1839, the regularly published *Journal of the Asiatic Society of Bengal* superseded in India William Jones's *Asiatick Researches*. In 1841, the Bombay branch published its own journal. A year later the American Oriental Society was founded and a journal soon followed. And in 1847, the *Zeitschrift der deutschen morgenlandis-*

chen Gesellschaft was launched in Leipzig, published by the German Oriental Society (1845). From the second half of the eighteenth century, the Westernizing of Russia had prompted a certain outpouring of Orientalist works. Beginning in 1804, Russian universities began to offer Islamic languages in cities such as Kharkov and even more significantly at Kazan, in Muslim territory. As domestic policies were developed for the Muslim population, the center at Kazan became even more important.[119]

Thus, Orientalism was born. The term *Orientalist* appeared in English around 1779 and in French in 1799. The French form, *orientalisme*, found a place in the *Dictionnaire de l'Académie Française* of 1838. The idea of a particular discipline devoted to the study of the "Orient" was taking shape. As yet, however, there were not enough specialists to warrant forming associations or publishing journals exclusively devoted to one country, people or region of the East. The intellectual range of every scholar extended over several domains, not all of which could be studied with the same depth. From here on, one was simply an Orientalist.

The idea of Orientalism indicates a greater depth of study but also a withdrawal from and break with other studies. In eighteenth-century works of synthesis, the East took its place beside the West. Both were part of a universalist vision. Hereafter, it became clear that prior study based on original texts and a knowledge of Eastern languages were the prerequisites for any serious consideration of the East. Indeed, by this time such study meant an enormous amount of work. It encompassed among other things editing and translating texts, compilation of thoroughly researched dictionaries and grammars, exposition of narrative history, and so on. Specialists might well hold general ideas, but it was their responsibility to ensure that such generalities did not influence their own research. They also had little time to follow scientific advances outside their own field. The discipline of the human sciences was still very new; it lacked as yet a methodology precise enough to shape the enormous mass of received information into syntheses with a theoretical framework. Moreover, most philosophical doctrines were either too general or too implicitly ideological to be of much use in this effort.

The number of Orientalist institutions began to increase quite rapidly. Victor Hugo, in the preface to his collection of poems, *Les Orientales* (which opened with three epigraphs of Saʻdī and contained a series of translated Arabic and Persian poems), wrote:

Oriental studies have never been so advanced. In the age of Louis XIV, one was a Hellenist; now one is an Orientalist.... Never before have so many minds simultaneously worked so hard to bring to light this great darkness that is Asia. We now have specialists for every Oriental dialect from China to Egypt.

These scholars were a source of reliable information for artists and writers as well: Hugo, for example, consulted the Orientalists Ernest Fouinet (1799–1845) and the Baron Nicholas d'Eckstein (1790–1861); Goethe was indebted to the German philologist Friedrich Diez (1794–1876) and many others.

Literary and artistic Orientalism, of course, was encouraged by all the events concerning the Muslim East, especially the "Eastern Question," one of the burning issues facing Europe in the nineteenth century. The earliest expressions of this mode of Romantic exoticism date significantly from the Greek War of Independence. It was this event that inspired Byron (he died in Greece in 1824) as well as Delacroix, whose work the *Massacre at Chios*, the earliest example of an Orientalist painting, was first shown in Paris in that same year of 1824. What would become the Romantic vision of the East for years to come could already be seen in this picture and in Hugo's *Les Orientales* (the earliest poem in the collection dates from 1825). Indeed, these were the features that would capture the European imagination and fascinate such a widespread audience for years. The image was characterized by fierce and lavish scenes in a wild array of colors; harems and seraglios; decapitated bodies; women hurled into the Bosporus in sacks; feluccas and brigantines displaying the Crescent flag; round, turquoise domes and white minarets soaring to the heavens; viziers, eunuchs, and odalisques; refreshing springs under palm trees; *giaours* with their throats slit; captive women forced into submission by their lustful captors.[120] As the poet Heine (1797–1856) had already accurately noted, these daringly colorful paintings catered to the bourgeois European's baser instincts. The staid Westerner, disturbed by his own sexuality and beset by unconscious sado-masochistic tendencies, could find in this art a kind of easy gratification, a cheap thrill. Even when Westerners traveled to the East, it was this image they were really seeking; as a result, they chose sights with a merciless disregard for whatever did not conform to their predetermined vision of the world.

This image, tinged with European sensibility at its own stage of evolution, also reflected a real situation. The Muslim East was still an enemy in the nineteenth century, but an enemy doomed to defeat. In 1853, Czar Nicholas I, in conversation with the British naval commander Sir Hamilton Seymour, could speak of the "the sick man, seriously ill" that Europe had "on its hands," namely, the Ottoman Empire. Actually, it had been a very long time since European hegemony had been challenged. Since the eighteenth century, the withdrawal of the Turks had been conspicuous. With the independence of Greece in the 1800s, decline had reached the very core of the empire.

European colonization now began with the French taking Algiers in 1830 and the British establishing themselves in Aden in 1839. British control in distant India
and Malaysia now appeared as unshakeable as that of the
Dutch in Indonesia. All evidence seemed to indicate that
the East was destined for European domination, since it
was crumbling from within, a victim of its own neglect,
the West's long-awaited dream of Europeanizing this world
could now be accomplished. The ferocity of the East need
no longer instill fear and outrage. Instead, it was merely a
cultural trait that could entrance but offered no risk. It
was surely no small relief to concede the honors of war to
an enemy that had by then all but surrendered.

The lands of the East were now seen as the crumbling
remnants of a formerly great civilization. One could in-
dulge in the luxury of praising the East just as politicians
and businessmen were doing all they could to hasten its
decline. The possibility of its recovery or modernization
aroused no enthusiasm, for in the process, it might lose
the whiff of exoticism that lent charm. Such unromantic
plans upset poets and artists alike, and, through their influence, the greater public as well. Likewise, but for more
positive reasons, most of the political and economic leaders would also find this unpleasant, even if it were feasible.
The Oriental may always have been characterized as a sav-
age enemy, but during the Middle Ages, he was at least
considered on the same level as his European counterpart.
And, to the men of the Enlightenment, the ideologues of
the French revolution, the Oriental was, for all his foreign-
ness in appearance and dress, above all a man like anyone
else. In the nineteenth century, however, he became something quite separate, sealed off in his own specificity, yet
worthy of a kind of grudging admiration. This is the ori-
gin of the *homo islamicus*, a notion widely accepted even
today.

The theory that there were different civilizations, which were evolving in their own allotted space, was becoming universally accepted. But, while this concept of separate cultures was influenced by the wave of nationalist uprisings throughout Europe, it still remained a philosophical abstraction. The theory maintained that each civilization was unique, endowed with a particular, essential nature. To identify this essential feature, an increasing number of scholars began to forsake the study of recent periods and focus instead on earlier ages and what were considered the "purer" characteristics of "classical" civilizations. This trend in scholarship was further advanced by the two humanist sciences that were especially favored in the nineteenth century: the history of religions and the study of historical and comparative linguistics.

The history of religions grew out of the struggle between bourgeois relativist pluralism and the ideological monopoly of Christianity. It stimulated great interest in the study of Eastern religions as alternatives to Christianity both in the past and in the present. As part of the era's underlying theoretical idealism, the new historians of religion inculcated the idea that the essence of each civilization is spiritual: religion permeates and explains every aspect of a civilization. These conclusions are also connected to issues raised by historical and comparative linguistics, as initiated by Franz Bopp (1791–1867), the German philologist and student of Silvestre de Sacy. The result of the work done by Bopp and his followers (which aroused great interest) was to give to language, indeed to each specific language, a key rôle. A people was assumed to identify with its language; it could be defined by its particular linguistic features. If languages could be related to one another, then a similar relationship could exist between the spirits of different peoples (*Volkgeister*), an interconnection on the deepest level. It was held that this spirit of a people explained all the social features discernible in its history. With biological evolutionism and the new field of physical anthropology, interest also turned to the classification of races. Such work gained immediate prestige and wide acceptance because it adopted the scientific method used in the natural sciences. As with religion and language, the concept of race was seen as an essential quality, only in this case, one endowed with a particular strength.

The increasing pressure to specialize, however, precluded any real appreciation of the contributions of these new sciences. It was only in the most oversimplified and unimaginative versions that these developments reached scientists in other fields. For example, what amounted to the entire study of Eastern civilizations was left to the philologists. The problem was that, lacking a theoretical framework of their own (aside from the study of texts, textual criticism, etc.), they could only reflect the common opinions of their own society in their appreciation of the social and historical factors.

Thus, despite the tremendous amount of accurate information and precise documentation, which the specialists were able to assemble, the rift between their intellectual efforts and the world of objective reality continued to widen. Their learning was undoubtedly substantial, yet it focused on a view of a cultural whole that had now disappeared as such, but to which was attributed an immutable, underlying influence. This vision was shaped by the most general ideas of the time, which transmitted in their popularized forms, the findings of the history of religions, historical linguistics, and physical anthropology so that the power of religion, language, and race was magnified beyond all proportion. The actual problems of contemporary Oriental societies were totally ignored: such matters were considered undignified and best left to the reports of merchants, travelers, diplomats, and economists.

In the eighteenth century, the purpose of theoretical knowledge was to bring the average man closer to an understanding of his own time. However, it can be said in a very general sort of way that the work of nineteenth and early twentieth-century scholars was only minimally concerned with the contemporary world. Moreover, their rare ventures into the concerns of the present were usually misguided, influenced more by current prejudices than scientific research. Consequently, there were some who were so overawed by the great erudition of these scholars that they accepted their conclusions without question and thus went on to commit serious errors themselves. It was certainly a genuine erudition, but nonetheless limited and colored by the scholars' own prejudices. Conversely, the ascetic ethics of textual criticism still enforced after about 1850, came under the influence of positivism and scientism resulting in much stricter standards for factual documentation and the theoretical conclusions from these facts. In reality, however, this ideal kind of research was often undercut when scholars actually organized their information. In their reading of this data, they continued to rely on the prevalent assumptions of their own society, thereby unwittingly biasing their own conclusions.

Diplomats, technicians, and economists, when the circumstances were more or less favorable, had a less abstract view of the countries of the Muslim East and were occasionally able to see them as societies in transition, which could, under the right conditions, move forward and develop. Such was the case for Muḥammad ʻAlī's Egypt, which excited some enthusiasm in France within the framework of its anti-British policy. For the most part, exoticism merely led to a nostalgia for the past and a fear of European-style modernization. But, paradoxically, and perhaps indirectly, this same exoticism led others who had a passionate and sincere interest in the countries concerned to opt for progress and, as a result, to pay more attention to the social evolution taking place in the Middle East. Here again, there was a parting of the ways, and several courses were open. Some envisioned the desired evolution as being directed by their own European homeland (Lyautey, Massignon, T. E. Lawrence, at first). Others (W. S. Blunt) stood in opposition to such sentiments of nationalistic domination. Between these two extremes were a whole range of intermediate positions, and some even changed their own position over time.

These ideas often reflected general conceptions of the apologetic kind past and present. Thus, in the late 1800s, some French writers, through a curious mixture of theoretical anti-colonialism and anglophobic patriotism, were able to paint a rosy picture of the Sudan under Muḥammad Aḥmad, the self-styled Madhi. The general notions of the day once again tended to give a twist to ideas. When the English poet W. S. Blunt (1840–1922) devised plans to restore the Arab world and Islam by a partial and modified return to medieval forms, he actually provided very important material that would be appropriated and reworked by the first theorists of Muslim and Arab nationalism.

From the mid-nineteenth century on, one phenomenon more than any other determined the European image of the East, and that was imperialism. The economic, technical, military, political, and cultural dominance of the West was decisive, while the underdeveloped East continued to founder. Iran and the Ottoman Empire were becoming little more than European protectorates. Outright colonization began to spread chiefly after 1881, the date of the occupation of Tunisia and Egypt. It had expanded into Central Asia to the advantage of the Russians, and in the Maghrib and the Ottoman East, in favor of the English, French, and Italians. This inevitably reinforced an already well-established Eurocentrism, which took on a very markedly contemptuous tinge.

In the eighteenth century, an unconscious sense of Eurocentrism was present but it was guided by the universalist ideology of the Enlightenment and therefore respected non-European civilizations and peoples. With good reason it discovered universal human traits in their historical development and their contemporary social structures. But with a kind of pre-critical naïveté, eighteenth-century scholars attributed to these civilizations the same underlying bases as European civilization. Any cultural specificity was only superficially recognized. The conscious and intellectually-developed Eurocentrism erred in the opposite direction. An irreducible specificity was assumed at all possible levels; universal motivations and traits were denied or belittled. If there was to be any universality at all, it would have to be based entirely on the European model. Its adoption may have been considered necessary, but its realization was in fact deemed impossible, given the acute specificity of non-European peoples. For this reason, such universality remained little more than an ideal. With this recognition, it became evident that any real Westernization would have to be postponed until some vague future date. For the present, the exotic cultures of the East would have to remain in their degraded and politically dominated status.

Moreover, some Easterners themselves seemed to lend credence to this assessment of the situation by adopting the European model, starting with its most superficial aspects, while others totally rejected it and continued to adhere to the most archaic values of their own culture, although these had often been renewed from within. Mass demonstrations and mob violence against the spread of

European influence were disparagingly written off as eternally recurring manifestations of Muslim fanaticism and nothing more. Research on the classical periods intensified and produced a growing number of specialized studies. In their work, scholars noted, with an understandable bias, any indications of classical culture that remained operative in their own time. In so doing, consciously or not, they often lent the weight of their scientific authority to such a presentation of things.[121]

The degraded state of the Muslim world made it an obvious target for Christian missionaries. The proselytizing crusade was launched with renewed vigor and quickly spread, impatiently contending with the strictures of Muslim law and the concerns of colonial authorities as to the repercussions such missionary activity might provoke. In keeping with the common beliefs of their time and normal human inclinations, the missionaries credited the triumphs of European nations to Christianity while blaming the misfortunes of the Muslim world on Islam. The perception was that, if Christianity was inherently favorable to progress, then Islam must, by its nature, encourage cultural and developmental stagnation.

The campaign against Islam became as fierce as ever, fortified as before with arguments dating back to the Middle Ages, but with modern embellishments. As a result, passing references to the satanic foundation of Islam now occasionally appeared. French Catholics, for example, claimed that a conspiracy was uniting against progress and truth (as represented by the Church). Furthermore, the conspirators in this case, were not only Muslims, but Protestants, Englishmen, Freemasons, and Jews, all obedient to Satan. The Muslim religious orders were considered particularly dangerous and were believed to be inspired by a virulent hatred of civilization.[122] Paradoxically, it is worth noting that similar conclusions can be found in the work of anti-clerics in the Voltaire tradition. They worshiped Hellenism, as a civilization founded on the freedom of the spirit, the worship of reason and beauty, and inspired by the same Aryan spirit as the Vedas, the source of European greatness. In opposition to this, they envisioned a Semitic spirit of intolerance, scholastic dogmatism, fanatical and blind reliance on faith alone, a debilitating fatalism, and a contempt for the visual arts. Attributed to this spirit were all the misdeeds associated with Judaism, Christianity, and Islam.[123]

In much the same way and at the same time as the Yellow Peril, pan-Islam was becoming a fashionable bogey. A triumphant Europe saw all resistance to its domination as a sinister conspiracy. Such a plot could only be inspired by a cruel, Machiavellian spirit. In light of the perpetually recurring psychological workings in the history of ideologies, one was apt to see there an illusory unity of purpose and a meticulous attention to the execution of evil designs that relied on the most treacherous methods to oppose the Europeans. Whenever there was any show of anti-imperialism, even if it was a purely local reaction, pan-Islam was blamed.[124] The very word itself suggested an attempt at domination, aggressive ideology, and international conspiracy. Through the popular press, popular literature, and even children's books, this view had a lasting effect on the thinking of many Europeans. It also influenced scholars, particularly when they went so far as to give their supposedly competent advice to overseers of colonial policies. For those scholars who ventured into current events, like the Dutch scholar and administrator Snouck Hurgronje (1857–1936) and Carl Heinrich Becker (1876–1933), who was for a time the Prussian secretary of state, pan-Islam became something of an obsession. Analyzing it with varying degrees of subtlety, they tended to see it as an essentially reactionary phenomenon. Without yielding to all the popular assumptions, these scholars nonetheless were inclined to see in what were actually loose and widely divergent tendencies far more unity and organization than there really was.[125] Moreover, their very erudition tended to focus almost all of their attention on a single problem, namely, the real, but hardly inevitable, danger posed by a return in the East to an earlier theocratic state. Adhering to this single archaic vision, they not only devalued other active social forces present in the Middle East, but, by their contempt, encouraged these social forces to pursue a reactionary course. In short, these scholars were once again irresistibly drawn to a vision of the East that hearkened back to the Middle Ages: the struggle was still between two politically and ideologically opposed worlds.

Most specialists, however, had no interest in these problems and were content to adopt the prevailing views whenever they had to deal with issues outside their particular area of expertise. They were often slow to accept any new attitudes or methodology. Philological bias continued to dominate Oriental studies. A wealth of scientific material became available and research methods became more and more rigorous. Communication between scholars increased and became better organized, developing even on the worldwide scale, with international conferences of Orientalist scholars, the first of which was held in Paris in 1873. Yet, if there was any progress in the understanding of societies, cultures, and ideas, it was due entirely to the intellectual achievement of a few remarkable scholars.

The slow emergence of the social and human sciences had, as yet, little effect on all of this. Most Middle Eastern specialists showed no particular interest in sociology, psychology, demography or political economy: for their purposes, such disciplines seemed quite irrelevant. Conversely, the first sociologists considered the study of the Middle East an integral part of their own research. Their concern however was either with the classical Muslim world or with ancient customs and traditions still practiced in the modern Muslim world. More often than not, sociologists made the wise decision not to probe too deeply into areas so foreign to their understanding and, in fact, they deferred instead to the Islamists for their information. Islamists themselves, trained mainly in philological matters, as was usual, may have accepted certain new ideas launched by the first sociologists, but none of them acquired the specialized training and knowledge of real sociologists.

The influence of new and energetic disciplines was especially evident in the ethnography of the Muslim peoples. This influence resulted in such remarkable works as those of Edmond Doutté (e.g., *Magie et religion dans l'Afrique du Nord*, 1908) and Edward Westermarck (e.g., *Marriage Ceremonies in Morocco*, 1914). The modern development of Muslim nations was not considered an important subject of scholarly inquiry and was disdainfully relegated to people such as economists, journalists, diplomats, military men, and amateurs. Moreover, there was a tendency to reduce any examination of the modern Muslim world to a narrow focus on whatever remained from the past. As sociologists began to undertake direct empirical research, most of them, lacking any prior philological training, turned to the study of European and American society for their data. Curiously, because of this, the word sociology itself tended to be restricted to the study of those societies.

Without the complex theoretical framework necessary to interpret social structures and developments, history, in the Oriental field as elsewhere, remained essentially descriptive. Even so, historical scholarship was revitalized by the work of earlier historians like Barthold Georg Niebuhr

(1776–1831; son of Carsten Niebuhr, noted for his travels
to Arabia) and the German historian Leopold von Ranke
(1795–1886), both of whom applied rigorous standards to
the analysis of source materials. Orientalist historians like
Gustav Weil (1808–89), Aloys Sprenger (1813–93), Rein-
hart Dozy (1820–83), and Michele Amari (1806–89) followed the same pattern; they were rigorous in presenting
factual information only after conscientious research. They
were open-minded in principle, free from any theoretical
preconception about the nature of the historical factors,
but, in fact, heavily influenced by the prevailing ideas of
their time. Thus Sprenger, whose critical approach in his
Das Leben und die Lehre des Mohammed (1861–65) led
to a revised history of the Prophet, was influenced by the
Hegelian concept of the *Zeitgeist*. Among the Orientalist scholars, Alfred von Kremer (1828–89) was probably
the first to see the history of Islam as an integral whole.
To him, it was the influence of dominant ideas that provided the "key to understanding the religious and social
systems of Islam." [126] Most specialists accepted the general
idea—one that often remained implicit—that religious and
ideational factors were predominant.

The school of French historians that flourished between
1820 and 1850 based its analysis on the internal dynamics operating between social groups in conflict. This view,
however, had no influence among Orientalist scholars for
whom the essential conflicts were between "races" and religions. (It could be added, for example,, that the historian Augustin Thierry [1795–1856] identified class struggles with these conflicts between "races.") Thus, Shīʿism
was usually explained as a reaction of the Persian, Aryan
spirit against the Semitic spirit of Islam.

However, aware of the social conflicts of his time, the
philologist Hubert Grimme (1864–1942), in his *Mohammed*
(1892–95), was the first to examine, albeit superficially,

the key rôle of social factors in the life of the Prophet.
A more elaborate analysis came from the German Protestant theologian Julius Wellhausen (1844–1918), renowned
as a Biblical critic and a historian of ancient Israel. In his
Die religiös-politischen Oppositionsparteien im alten Islam
(1901), he emphasized the rise of religious schisms and the
succession of dynasties in the early days of Islam as evinc-
ing the dynamism of political and social conflict. C. H.
Becker pursued similar lines in his *Islamstudien* (1924–
32), and Leone Caetani (1869-1935), for example, in his
Studia di storia orientale (1914), went even further in his
appeal to economic factors. Thus, influenced by the concerns prevalent at the beginning of the twentieth century,
there was a tendency to question the habitual eclectic positivism of the time, not by replacing it with any general
theoretical analysis of social structures and dynamics, but
by simply transposing and emphasizing the predominant
factors of the contemporary European world. For the most
part, specialists questioned these attempts, some of which
were indeed excessive and open to criticism. And, as a
result, they preferred to maintain a cautiously aloof and
decidedly academic agnosticism.

Challenges to Eurocentrism

In the field of Oriental studies, as in other fields, the First
World War shattered the self-confident belief of European
civilization in the continuity and limitlessness of its own
progress, and in so doing, shook European ethnocentrism.
What seemed like an unassailable supremacy could now be
challenged by national uprisings, such as the Arab revolt
in the East (even if channeled), the Kemalist movement
in Turkey, the growing unrest throughout the diverse nations of Imperial Russia, and insurrections in India and
Indonesia (all as a continuation of the Iranian and Young

Turk revolutions of the 1905–14 period). The conventional
explanation was that, if European authority was indeed
in jeopardy, it was obviously the work of a wicked conspiracy against Good. In this case, the specter of Russian
Bolshevism was to blame, conveniently reinforcing the already traditional rôle of satanic Freemasonry and the per-
versions of Catholic, Jewish or Protestant religions, de-
pending on the writer's belief and the particular revolt in
question.

In the years immediately following the war, Oswald
Spengler produced his glittering work, *The Decline of the
West* (1918–22). *The Rising Tide of Color against White
World-Supremacy* by the American writer Theodore Lothrop Stoddard appeared in 1920. A year later, even more
pointedly, he published *The New World of Islam*. Stoddard was certainly no scholar but he was a rather well-
informed apologist for the West, who, without denying his
own racist viewpoint, showed that because of profound
changes, "this strange new East which now faces us is
mainly the result of Western influences."[127] His image of
the "new East" was essentially that of a world revolving
around a mysterious, fundamentally different, hostile, and
rather repugnant nucleus composed of an ignorance and
savagery that was only barely restrained by religion, custom, and a small enlightened élite.[128] On closer examination, however, many of the factors that Stoddard identified
as prevalent in the East were equally operative throughout Western history. For instance, the struggle against
oppression and foreign interference as well as the aspirations of the lower social classes to a better life were both
expressed, interpreted, and reflected by different ideologies.

This remained the overall view shared by the European
and American public, including most scholars. However,
the emphasis was placed on the first factor—the latent

and inadequately restrained savagery, the fanaticism that had been unleashed against the civilizing advance from the West.

This undermining could not fail to have its effect. The personality and work of T. E. Lawrence (1888–1935), present a dramatic example of the collision between romantic exoticism and a reality that was understood in its universal aspects but was still suffused with the magic of local color. For some Turcophiles, following the example of the French novelist Pierre Loti (1850–1923) exoticism was the first step toward a genuine understanding of native aspirations. More often, however, the anti-colonialists were universalists who had little interest in the past or in the specific characteristics of the present, which they considered remnants of a barbarous past best destroyed. Exoticism, rather, prompted colonial officials to leave any archaic features untouched, to ally themselves with indigenous conservatives, and to denounce the nationalist intellectuals—whether reformists, or revolutionaries, socialists or not—as feeble imitators of Europe, who were driven to destroy their own heritage by abstract, ill-digested ideas. In general, this was also the verdict of the public at large. Modernization was considered an inauthentic element, a betrayal of the East's individuality.

A rather similar view of the East was shared by European esoterists. They sought in the Muslim East, as well as, for example, in the Buddhist East, a model for the wise life, a contact with supra-sensory realities and with ancestral secrets handed down by a long line of initiates. Far from attributing satanic inspiration to the Muslim brotherhoods, they saw in them cells through which was transmitted the ancestral theosophical tradition. Some, like the French philosopher René Guénon (1886–1951), actually converted to Islam and died Muslims. In Europe and America, this spiritual trend and fabulous vision of an esoteric Islam accounted for the success of numerous sects, which were inspired to varying degrees by Islam and (even allowing for all sorts of misunderstandings) by orthodox Islam and by a religion such as Bahaism.

Marxism, the dissident voice that split Europe and transformed Russia, had only a modest influence on the ideas of the anti-colonialist liberalism that was the legacy of the French revolution. As theoretical Marxism was popularized in a schematic, oversimplified form and treated as an ideology in the service of established institutions, it tended to minimize the rôle of ideological superstructures. As a result, the Muslim world, for example, was seen merely as a part of the greater underdeveloped world, which European capitalism oppressed and exploited. According to this view, the Muslims shared exactly the same aspirations as other groups. Among their own people there were oppressors ("feudal" or bourgeois) who exploited the populace. The masses, once relieved of their prejudices and in possession of the necessary lucidity, were just as likely to revolt as were any other oppressed people. This awareness would arise naturally from the regenerating forces of the indigenous proletariat. Due to the extreme weakness of the industrial proletariat in these countries, the leadership would fall to those scarce and very exiguous communist cells that were supposed to embody the essence of the theoretical and strategic thinking of the worldwide proletariat. Communists in advanced Western nations (especially those with colonies) were not immune from the attitudes of their compatriots. From their perspective, the Muslims remained culturally backward because of the strength of fanaticism, which these Western Marxists saw as an intrinsic part of Islam. To be sure, the Muslims would eventually become enlightened but while awaiting this development in consciousness, the revolutionary rôle, even in Muslim countries, belonged to the European élite.[129]

To Russian Communist leaders inside the Soviet Union, the Muslims were simply a group of people who were particularly susceptible to reactionary ideas. The first step toward understanding the Muslims was to dispel all the exotically inspired sentimentality about Islam.[130] With the extinction of "feudal" and bourgeois elements and the establishment of the necessary bases for a socialist economy, their earlier prejudices would gradually disappear with the help and enlightenment of the Russian Big Brother, who was more advanced in these matters. Of course, all religions were to be eradicated and Islam was no exception, although provisional phases or tactical compromises in the anti-religious struggle were considered acceptable. The Muslim peoples, of course, had their own national cultures and these were to be preserved, provided they took on a socialist content and were purged of all religious elements.

Outlines of more subtle appreciations appeared early, but they hardly emerged at the explicit and theoretical levels. For example, from the outset of the Soviet regime, the Tatar communist, Sultan Galiev (ca. 1880–1940), had argued that the Muslim world was, by virtue of qualities unique to Islam, particularly susceptible to communism and the spread of communist ideology. This being the case, he reasoned there was obviously no need to attack or destroy Islam. But, Galiev met with official disfavor and was brutally ousted from the Communist Party. It was only outside the Soviet Union, and mainly in Indonesia and the Arab nations, that other communists embraced his ideas, though very timidly and then only after quite some time.[131] Actually, many who shared Galiev's views left the communist fold to become nationalists, though still with Marxist or simply socialist leanings.[132]

The image of the Muslim world was further modified, at least in certain limited but influential sectors of Western society, by the inexorable wave of anti-colonialist activity. Political and commercial leaders in the West could also appreciate the struggle for independence in the East. At least on its purely nationalistic level, it was represented by upper-class Muslims who were eager to adapt themselves to the West in order to acquire the dynamic and dominating virtues of free enterprise. From the perspective of a kind of universalist capitalism, the Muslims were no different from any other group: they could follow the same path as had white Europeans and Americans since the nineteenth century. This was, in part, the position of the English writer Freya Stark, whose 1945 work was appropriately entitled *East Is West*. In direct opposition to Kipling's imperialist and exoticist attitudes, she dedicated the book to "her brothers, the young effendis." Of course, she still took into account local peculiarities but in her view, they were of secondary importance. As for Islam, it was seen to have the same rôle as any other religion: it could provide its followers with spiritual reasons for living, without obstructing their economic activity. In fact, it could even serve as a bulwark against the ravages of atheistic communist ideology.

Naturally, left-wing anti-colonialism was an entirely different matter. The universalism that it derived from its liberal or socialist roots tended to change into a recognition, and ultimately, even an exultation of individuality. Now, it was in the Third World that the exploited, oppressed, and brutalized element with its crude strength would, once and for all, overthrow the misery and domination of the old order. From then on, those values intrinsic to the formerly colonized peoples were to receive due praise, which was not diminished even when very normal misunderstandings resulted in the discovery, albeit in specific forms, that the very same values animated the European groups concerned. To some of those who were more deeply committed in this direction, Islam itself was seen as an inherently "progressive" force. There were even conversions to Islam.

This tendency reached its most extraordinary expression with a group of left-wing Catholics led by the very learned French scholar Louis Massignon (1883–1962). Imbued with a mystical view of history and rooted in the centuries-old Christian tradition of devotion to the poor and humble, he carried to extremes the latent tendency of Christianity of recent times, which has found its clearest and most forceful exponents in the Roman Catholic Church. The threat of atheism, the revision of traditional points of view whose responsibility for the dechristianization of the Western masses seems obvious, the return to the fundamental and original values of the Christian faith, have all brought about a feeling of solidarity with, rather than hostility toward, other religions. The ecumenical movement, while not relinquishing the claim that the Church is in possession of the whole truth and that its ambition is to bring the wayward back to that truth, has nevertheless renounced extra-spiritual pressure and realized that the upholders of other beliefs are partners in debate and eventual allies, that they are men of good faith devoted to values worthy of respect, who no longer can be considered satanic foes to be annihilated.

In October 1965, the Ecumenical Council of Vatican II paid tribute to Islam for the "truths" it helped to impart about God and His power, Jesus, Mary, the prophets, and the apostles. In the Middle Ages, these truths were deemed merely façades used to cover the fundamental Islamic imposture as it attempted to gain admission. People are now coming to the opinion that Muslim "errors" are of doubt-

ful importance next to the central monotheistic message
proclaimed by Islam.

With this ideological about-face, the Christian position on Muhammad has become a sensitive issue. It is
hardly possible any longer, as it was in the Middle Ages,
to see him as a sheer satanic impostor. While the majority
of Christian ideologues concerned with this matter may
wisely reserve their judgment about Muhammad, some
Roman Catholic scholars of Islam consider him a "religious genius." Others go even further and have wondered
whether Muhammad might not be a true prophet, given
that St. Thomas Aquinas speaks of a kind of directive
prophecy that does not require the prophet to be infallible
or without sin.[133]

Some Christians, like Massignon, have been struck by
the spiritual value of Muslim religious experiences and disturbed by the historical injustices inflicted by their own
people against Islam, both as a religion and a group of peoples so recently oppressed and despised. They accordingly
have been led to formulate opinions that might justify the
charges of syncretism and "Islamizing heresy" that have
been hurled at them by outraged supporters of Church
integrity.[134]

In so doing, the anti-colonialists, whether or not Christian or leftist, often go so far as to practically sanctify Islam and the contemporary ideologies of the Muslim world,
thereby going from one extreme to an other. To a historian
like Norman Daniel, for example, only a mind tainted by
medievalism or imperialism could criticize the moral attitudes of the Prophet, and he accuses as being the same sort
of thing, any exposition that uses the normal mechanisms
of human history to explain Islam and its characteristics.
Understanding has given way to apologetics. The enthusiasm of these apologists is tempered only by the tendency
(often equally excessive) among some of them to honor

other ethnic, quasi-ethnic or religious groups with whom the Muslim world was or is in conflict—primarily black Africans and Jews.

This major reconciliation has met resistance among certain segments of European-American popular opinion. There are those elements just mentioned as well as Christian fundamentalists, generally of rightist leanings, who maintain medieval or imperialist attitudes and remain determined to defend Christian and European civilization against the rising tide of Muslim barbarianism. As for specialist scholars, they are either indifferent or divided between these various tendencies, with all their subtle nuances.

The range of new problems and issues addressed by the human sciences was finally taken up by Orientalist scholars. A growing number of specialists, whether their focus was on the medieval Muslim world or more recent periods, approach the problems from the sociological angle.[135] More and more scholars have also embraced the long-neglected fields of economic and social history.[136] There has, in fact, been an effort in all areas of Islamic studies to go beyond purely philological research. Scholars now attempt at least partial syntheses that are no longer based on simple common sense or philosophical generalities. They now try to make use of the results achieved by scholars working in a chosen field of social phenomena: historians who study a coherent group of phenomena, demographers, economists, sociologists, and so on.

Furthermore, there has been a concurrent increase in contacts with native scholars. For a long time, the main obstacle was the dearth of specialists who had freed themselves from the medieval modes of study and thought. In the past, collaborators in these fields were often merely informants whose contributions had to be totally rethought by European scholars. The social obstacles to the setting up of truly specialized research teams were, in part, the colonial status of the Muslim East and in part, the rôle of social and cultural traditions.[137] These difficulties have only partially been overcome. Other problems have arisen, largely out of the vigor of ideological options open to the Muslim world at a time of bitter struggle against the vestiges of European domination. Such times tend to yield to ideological extremism. European scholars frequently shy away from this extremism without always understanding their motives and overlooking the ideological components of their own judgments. But, the obstacle is serious, even though it could be easily overcome in research bearing on narrow and well-defined points where neither religious nor nationalist ideology could possibly be an issue.[138]

Another general and unmistakable trend is the growing interest in what used to be contemptuously referred to as the "low periods" of history.[139] A cultural essentialism, stressing the supremacy of religion and "race" and positing the existence and durability of a "pure" type for each civilization, had made the study of the Muslim Middle Ages the preferred area of scholarship. Under the influence of economic and social research, of the new sociological orientation, of contacts with economists, demographers, and anthropologists, a great interest is now taken in the study of more recent periods, a situation encouraged by the much more plentiful documentation. It has to be remembered that the Ottoman Empire, Safavid Persia, and the great Mughal empire marked the height of Islam.[140] Even the period of close contacts with the West and the emergence of modern ideologies present problems, which, though more or less modern, are not on that account, inconsequential or contemptible.

As in the other human sciences, the current view is that problems must be defined, discussed, and illuminated from every possible angle. This requires a multidisciplinary

approach and excludes the artificial hierarchy between dig-
nified and undignified disciplines. Concern over the gath-
ering, collation, and indexing of research materials prepared and presented in the best way possible (never an
exclusive concern) is giving way to a tendency toward rational discussion of problems. Both styles have their advantages and disadvantages. Ascetic rigorism, which occasionally led to an overly narrow perspective, has been
followed by grander visions that may result in insubstan-
tial drivel. Such a course may endanger the very necessary
task of publishing basic documents, which await, in overwhelming numbers, to be edited, collated, and indexed.
It is true, however, that modern techniques give reason
for some hope that these materials will be handled more
rapidly, but this could happen only within certain limits.

Some have even spoken of the end of Orientalism. The
issue must, however, be examined with subtle discrimination. There does not exist an Orientalist "science" whose
limits have been defined by God or by the nature of things.
What does exist is a multiplicity of issues coming under
the jurisdiction of many general disciplines. These issues
emerge from varied phenomena found in certain countries
previously grouped under the questionable rubric of the
East.

What is now at stake is the end of the dominance of
philology. The implicit belief, prevalent for more than a
century, that philological training is sufficient to deal com-
petently with all the problems within linguistically defined
areas is beginning to be abandoned. This notion, which
cannot be maintained on rational grounds, sprang from
the pressing need of a philological education for any serious study of the problems posed within a field. The vast
increase in accessible material, research tools, and progress
in methods of study now permit one, if not to pass over

the philological stage, at least to devote less time to it. Advances in the human sciences have also underscored the complexity of issues, which cannot be solved merely by a profound knowledge of language, by common sense, or eventually by the inspiration of very general philosophical ideas. The pursuit of Oriental studies, and especially Islamic studies, has, therefore, become more complex and less isolated. Contact with other disciplines, once considered a luxury, is now an urgent necessity. The promise for progress is impressive. The price to be paid is not too high.

Toward a New Approach to Arab and Islamic Studies

A cursory view of recent European scholarship on the Middle East reveals a wide-ranging diversity within the field—an impression that is frequently reinforced by the many scholars who insist their particular approach is different from that of their colleagues. Taken as a whole, however, all of these scholars share an unmistakable historical foundation and are subject to the same problems, given their common situation and intellectual orientation. These traits, common to all European scholarship, result from factors that can be divided into three general areas. First, there is a general human tendency, common to the most diverse societies (even at their most embryonic level) to study cultures and societies different from one's own. This general trend, regardless of how it must be explained, is submitted to certain cultural restraints, which are more or less different in every society. These constraints, in turn, are a function of (a) the social needs of each society (in this case, the same social requirements are shared in all European societies); (b) the general intellectual categories informing scientific research (these too are shared by most European societies); and (c) the insti-

tutions established within each society to serve as centers
for scientific inquiry (again these institutions are much the
same throughout Europe). Next, consideration must be
given to the internal trends dominating the evolution of
the mind-set, sensibilities, and values of an observer society (here, Europe). These trends can be characterized as
latent ideologies. It should be pointed out that this evolution is more or less common throughout Europe. Finally,
changes in the situation of the observer society with respect to the studied society will have an impact as well.
Here, once again, this process is common to all of Europe.

Moreover, given this background common to all European scholarship, specific national characteristics can be
easily identified. Their basis is: social demands, different
in each country; the specific developments for each of the
latter in teaching and research institutions; the particular
attitudes, values, mind-sets, and sensibilities prevailing in
each, which translate into different ideologies, implicit or
explicit; and the political, commercial, and other relationships that exist between each European nation and the
Muslim world.

Such differences, whether common to all of Europe or
unique only to certain countries, do not necessarily invali-
date the idea of a universally applicable and ideal scientific method for conducting research. The full realization
of this ideal methodology, however, remains elusive, like
a geometric asymptote. The inherent limitations and defi-
ciencies in earlier scholarly methodology become apparent
only gradually. An awareness of these limitations and of
the advance toward the realization of the ideal requirements arise from social conditions, shared attitudes, and a
collective mind-set from which the scholar cannot escape.
Yet, while these factors create new obstacles, they also offer new opportunities. It is important to keep all of these

factors and limitations in mind, or at least those that we are now capable of grasping.

Traditional Orientalism in the Past

The present state of affairs within the field of Islamic studies has its origins in a complete and relatively unified system of thought. I am unsure whether this system should be called *épistémé*, using Michel Foucault's term for systems more or less similar to this one. Actually, this sytem of thought, or collective scientific outlook, was formed by many different influences during the nineteenth century.

The most important contributing factor was the development of scientific research in the human sciences, which was itself related to the general advance of the scientific approach in all fields. All of nineteenth-century academe displayed an increased number of more and more specialized networks of research and teaching institutions. Moreover, this was accompanied by a continual demand for greater precision and objectivity in research itself.

Another significant factor in the development of nineteenth-century scholarship was the idea of expanding the field of Greco-Roman humanism to include civilizations outside the traditional sphere of classical study. This would bring to the field new sources of inspiration, imitation, and points of reference. This idea came out of a major shift in European sensibilities and attitudes as represented by the pre-Romantic and Romantic movements throughout nineteenth-century Europe. Romanticism, as is well known, focused on the specific, descriptive detail on the investigation of "national minds," each one with its specific traits, its local color, and so on. This romantic trend was a reaction against eighteenth-century universalism, which was based on the universal value of the Greco-Roman model. Obviously, despite this turning point

in European sensibilities, the earlier images of the Muslim
East persisted.

Here it is necessary to stress the importance of more
pragmatic types of contacts between the West and the
Muslim East. With the growing military, economic, and
political superiority that the Western world had by now
secured, contacts with the East increased in number and
intensity. During all this period, the general scholarly attitude of traditional Orientalism, as in all disciplines, was
what I would call "methodological restraint." In other
words, there was little tolerance of generalizations, which
were always considered premature, as for example, those
that were fashionable in earlier times and those that were,
at the same time, propounded by many writers and philosophers. The emphasis was, rather, on the idea that analysis must precede synthesis. Indeed, it was often said that
it would take years of analysis to come up with a single
hour of synthesis. This attitude may have been a thoroughly correct, fruitful, and valuable contribution to research, but it was coupled with the implicit, vague, and
far more dubious notion that synthesis would necessarily
be the natural result of any analysis. Furthermore, it was
felt that research should be a vast, collective enterprise
and that the individual scholar could only make a slight
contribution to that effort. As a result, the general trend
in research was toward a rigorous purism in scholarship
and a meticulous concern for precision. Clearly, there is
a connection between the rise of this stringent approach
to research and, in the area of economics, the developing
bourgeois ethic that Max Weber associated with Protes-
tanism.

The following passages are typical examples of this sort
of thinking in the field of Orientalism in the nineteenth
century. Both were written by Jules Mohl, secretary of
the Société Asiatique. The first is drawn from his very

valuable 1842 annual report to the society; the second was
written in 1841.

Toward the end of the last century, when it became clear that Oriental
literature was destined to extend human knowledge in an unforeseen
way that would incalculably benefit the history of religion, law, political institutions, and the arts, the study of that literature aroused a
general curiosity. Yet, science could not keep pace with the impatience
of those anxiously awaiting new revelations. The texts and translations that alone could provide a solid foundation for any further study
were slow to be published. Those who followed these developments
hoped for much but were only rewarded with fragments whose importance could not readily be ascertained since these fragments were
part of an immeasurably immense ensemble.[1]

And,

The urgency of publishing the major Oriental manuscripts cannot
be overemphasized. Only when scholars have focused their critical
attention on the masterpieces of each literary tradition, only when
printing has facilitated the circulation and use of these materials, ...
will the European intellect be able to truly penetrate the Orient,
to distinguish historical truth from the thick layer of fables and
contradictions that conceal it, and to reconstruct human history. We
are still far from this goal but the path is clearly marked and each
year we move toward it. Our progress may seem minimal if we look
at what remains before us; yet compared to what has been done, it is
considerable.[2]

As advanced by Mohl and others, this position is often
characterized (and not without some validity) as positivist.
It is, however, worth noting that Auguste Comte's original idea of positivism was little more than a philosophical
theory based on this general attitude toward methodological restraint. While it was not widely accepted by scholars,
positivism can be seen as a systematization and translation
of an implicit ideology. Indeed, perhaps "scientism" would
be a more accurate name for this ideology. It should, however, be emphasized that among scholars whose research

displayed this turn of mind, most showed no interest what-
soever in the metaphysical or philosophical implications
usually associated with the terms "positivism" or "scientism."

Among scholars, there was a growing awareness of the
magnitude of the task before them and, for most of them,
this inspired a gradual but concerted effort. A result of
this effort was the assembling of an immense body of acquired knowledge. For our purposes here, there is little
need to describe in detail how classical Orientalism came
to dominate this era by acquiring so much information.
A brief mention of some of the accomplishments will suf-
fice. Primary sources were deciphered, manuscripts were
catalogued, critically edited, annotated, and enriched by
learned commentaries. With the help of these sources, numerous research tools still in use today, such as bibliogra-
phies, tables, dictionaries, and grammars were published.
A further benefit of this research was the establishment
of a solid and reliable foundation for any future historical
work, including present-day scholarship. Examples of this
ground work include historical geography and factual history (although it is somewhat forgotten today how indispensable this approach remains, even if it is used in order
to go on to more advanced research models). The attitude
just described and the kind of work it produced, while
making a considerable advance, naturally was marked by
both personal virtues and shortcomings. These virtues
and failings are felt in the whole of scientific production
throughout the entire period.

It is essential to understand that this painstaking research (especially the study of remote languages and the
techniques for reading and transcribing manuscripts) required a long and difficult apprenticeship. Indeed, this
scholarship was so all-consuming (requiring, as it did, all
the time a person could possibly devote to any type of

work) that there was virtually no time left to become acquainted with general disciplines or specialists outside their field. Once these conditions are taken into account, it is easy to see how the philologist could almost completely dominate the field of Oriental studies in the nineteenth century.

These scholars shared, of course, the universal tendency among intellectuals of all times and places to formulate theories based on their own research. Such aspirations, however, were partly discouraged by the prevailing intellectual asceticism characterized by a strict adherence to the most minute detail. At other times, these aspirations were too easily satisfied, without the scholar exerting much effort. Most scholars relied on the prevailing ideas of their age, the current social consciousness, or their personal intuitions as isolated genius. In general, then, theories tended toward a certain eclecticism or, at times, to reflect the dominance of an attitude or interpretation then fashionable. To cite just one example: the crude "economism," which was inspired less by the limited influence of Marxism than by the meteoric rise of the industrial economy of the capitalist world, and which forms the basis of studies on the origins of Islam by scholars like Martin Hartmann and Leone Caetani.

Many scholars were eager to arrive at general conclusions, but because of their exceedingly specialized background, they were ill-equipped to do so. They attached far too much importance to the details and minor points of their own research and, as a result, they came up with syntheses that were often shaky or downright fanciful. Not surprisingly, more conscientious and aware scholars looked for inspiration, more narrowly and more wisely, to those social sciences that were relatively well-established by the mid-nineteenth century, namely, historical and comparative linguistics, the history of religions, and physical anthropology. But, the mechanical borrowing of ideas plucked from these limited fields, often produced disastrous results. Too often, the valid but invariably narrow findings from these sciences were rather incautiously applied to vast areas of human experience. For example, from what would become the extremely important field of the history of religions, nineteenth-century scholars appropriated the often implicit notion that ideas, and particularly religious ideas, utterly dominated the life of societies. Not unexpectedly, the result of this error was a kind of historical idealism. In the same way research on the genealogical classification of languages and the discoveries of physical anthropology were used to support a racist vision of society, despite the warnings and protestations of the scientists responsible for these findings. For example, even in the nineteenth century, many anthropologists expressed serious reservations about the value and use of cranial measurements as the basis for an artificial classification of race. Yet, there were distinguished scholars in other fields who completely disregarded these concerns and insisted, in their own historical research, on clear-cut distinctions between dolichocephalic and brachiocephalic peoples. In fact, even today, these types of racist conclusions can be found. Similarly, linguists in the nineteenth century warned against the fallacy of associating the speaker of a particular language with a given ethnic group. Of course, this too did not prevent the subsequent classification of peoples into groups such as Aryans and Semites, with their own eternal, immutable, and racially distinct characteristics. Once again, the influence of such facile theoretical formulations is still felt today. Thus, as great as the store of acquired knowledge was during the nineteenth century, its errors were of equal magnitude.

Then, too, there was the rôle of Eurocentrism. While, it may be pointless today to denounce this phenomenon and express righteous indignation at its legacy, it is still necessary to acknowledge it and to recognize its insidious influence. European society and civilization were held up as universally valid models assumed to be superior in all areas (European superiority, in fact, was real on a given level), but the factors active inside the fabric of Western society and civilization were taken out of context and rather mechanically applied to every society and era imaginable. Although certain specific factors may have been universal, this was by no means always the case. In general, the results of this wholesale transfer were extremely negative.

Moreover, still prevalent was the eighteenth-century notion that there were classical civilizations inherently superior to others, particularly during their "golden ages" and therefore the only eras worthy of serious scholarly attention. At the same time, this admiration for classical civilizations was coupled with an essentialist vision, namely, that each civilization was endowed with its own immutable essence. Scholars tended to seek this essential quality in the religion of the societies concerned. Thus, the essentialist vision was also a theologocentric one. To quote Jules Mohl again:

The influence of the four great literatures—Arab, Persian, Indian, and Chinese—also extends to the literatures of other Orientals. But, these peoples did not create centers of civilization, rather, they took their inspiration from one or more of these four greater nations. Therefore, one cannot expect to find in such secondary literatures the kind of epoch-making works that bear the stamp of original and creative spirit. Nor can one hope to see great numbers of scholars turn their attention to the study of these other literatures. But, it is to be hoped that these works will not remain unknown and that the knowledge they can provide to historians will be forthcoming. Indeed, these literatures may eventually come to light because of political and commerical needs to gather information about the Orient, or even through the efforts of a missionary or a man of letters. This information is invaluable because these peoples have their own historical records whose importance is in direct proportion to the level of their influence.[3]

Clearly, then, among the intellectual shortcomings of this period was the dependence on certain generalized notions of the nineteenth and early twentieth centuries: the pre-eminence and superiority of the European model, an often racist essentialism, and a frequently religious idealism.

Further connections could easily be established and developed. Brief mention at least should be made of the influence of both imperialist practices and "exoticist" aesthetic attitudes on intellectual theories of the period. Here again the point is not so much to denounce or condemn but to simply present the facts and understand their implications. Because of the lack of both a serious theoretical framework for the problems studied and any valid scientific program of research (i.e., of a sound problematics), much of the work of the period was seriously flawed. Of course, the importance of the immense body of information brought to light is not in question here. Indeed, to belittle this accumulation of data, as is often done today, is entirely groundless. True, many details were not illuminated at the time because the right questions were never asked. Nonetheless, a considerable amount of what was produced can still be used today as a basis for theories that researchers of earlier periods either could not or would not recognize.

Another essential failing of this era was the widespread (though unexpressed) trust in the omniscience of the philologist. For example, it was assumed that a specialist in Chinese language was perfectly capable of producing works on subjects such as Chinese philosophy, astronomy, and agriculture. Occasionally, these philologists turned out work that was good enough, but that was far from always the case. Clearly, this kind of scholarship is, at best, a risky business. Studies of this sort were often distinguished by their eclecticism and unawareness of the demands of methodology. What emerged was a kind of specialists' dilettantism. The pairing of these two words is not as contradictory as it may seem. The more a specialist narrows himself to his own area of expertise, the more likely he is to end up a dilettante when he presumes to explore areas outside of his competence.

The Present Crisis and Current Problems

The evolution of social mind-sets, new trends in thought, and changing circumstances have caused a fundamental crisis in the field of Islamic studies (among others) today. At the heart of this crisis is the development of the humanist or social sciences, which should have provided the foundation for considerable progress. A practical difficulty however remains. While the scholar in the field of Oriental studies must still have a good philological training, now it is imperative that he also be initiated into theoretical disciplines, such as sociology, etc., and this initiation is becoming more and more difficult. There are, however, limits to what one can do.

Another factor is the breakdown of Eurocentrism and the entry into the scientific fields of specialists from the very countries being studied. After decolonization and under the influence of anti-colonial sentiment, the great temptation in these countries now is to reject all the acquired knowledge of the preceding era as being tainted with Eurocentric and colonial attitudes. This is particularly the case for the generation of young students, professors, and teachers from formerly colonized nations. Regardless of how deeply one can sympathize with or understand the feelings that give rise to such a rejection, it must be pointed out that until now (for reasons having nothing to do with a presumed racial superiority), it has been the West alone that has applied the most refined scientific methods in its research, even if these methods had their practical beginnings in non-European civilizations.

Because of a well-intentioned desire to comply with the feelings of formerly oppressed peoples, at times even bordering on the obsequious, there is now commonly an emphasis on and deference toward a culture's own image and study of itself. The intimate knowledge of a society and its culture, which a member of that society enjoys, gives him an undeniably privileged position. We all have experienced this when looking at ourselves. However, it should not be forgotten that those outside the society also have certain advantages and indeed an outsider's distance from prevailing local ideologies is in itself a factor of utmost importance. This is especially the case during periods of intense conflict, such as the present, when the vision of participants involved in the struggle can easily be clouded by immediate political concerns.

Among the definitive and universally valid contributions of nineteenth- and twentieth-century European scientific research, one must, it seems to me, include the critical approach to primary sources. Although enlightened thinkers of other civilizations have occasionally used the same critical techniques, it was in Europe that these techniques were most completely developed and systematized. While such an approach is frequently denounced as callous to the sensibilities of non-European societies, it is essential to realize, and to underscore with some emphasis, that it was first applied in Europe and with regard to European sources. In the beginning, it was in the critical examination of the historical traditions on ancient Roman history and Biblical texts that new methods were elaborated, often disclaiming the truthfulness of the most revered sources.

Later these methods were continuously refined and perfected.

In the modern era, it has only been in Europe that a historical vision has been fully elaborated and universally applied. This has included a related phenomenon— the recognition of cultural pluralism and its consequences. Whatever the abuses associated with historicism, it did represent a major step forward. This single concept is a powerful weapon against the natural inclination to reconstruct the past in the image of the present and to project the mechanisms of our culture onto different cultural worlds. This rather automatic and naïve tendency is constantly reinforced by the new ideological constructs— chiefly political—that continually have a negative effect in many circles on a correct understanding of the social world. The only solution is to appeal to the historical spirit and return to original sources to counter the insidious influence these ideologies have on historical, ethnological or anthropological research in particular. It should be noted that in their current political struggles, the nationalist ideologies of most Third World countries naturally further tendencies opposed to the historical spirit.

Furthermore, the complete separation of scholarship from religious dogmatism was achieved for the first time in the modern Western world. Indeed, the entire scientific community, including those committed to religious beliefs, resolved in their research to divorce the supernatural from historical and sociological analysis. In studying sacred texts and histories, it was the European scientific community alone that was bold enough to apply only the laws governing human society.

In the field of linguistics, too, nineteenth-century Europe produced a revolution of Copernican proportions. This is in no way meant to deny or belittle the efforts of earlier Indian, Greek, Arab, and European, pre-modern grammarians whose work displayed acute insights into their own languages, sometimes even with genius. It was quite right, for example, that Noam Chomsky rehabilitated the "Cartesian linguistics" of the seventeenth-century Port Royal Jansenists. Nevertheless, in the nineteenth century, it was the Europeans alone who conceived of language as a dynamic system and who discarded the conception of immutable normative rules that governed earlier linguistic studies. They also sought to demystify languages of labels such as "sacred" and "classical" and to demonstrate the need for an objective study of all linguistic phenomena no matter how common or "vulgar." Moreover, they were able to clearly show that those languages that were written, taught, and studied were the superstructures of spoken languages and that the written language only followed and lagged behind the profound evolution affecting systems of phonemes, of grammatical forms, of syntactic patterns, and of lexical units of spoken languages. This approach represents a revolutionary advance that has not yet been entirely assimilated by the Arab East. Its importance cannot be overestimated. The structuralist study of language, dating back to the great Swiss linguist Ferdinand de Saussure (1857–1913), and now universally admitted, tends to minimize and even ignore this earlier advance. Yet without this contribution, it is clear that neither structuralist nor any other kind of linguistics would be possible.

The traditional Orientalists, more often than not, have reacted to this crisis with blind resistance and a certain inflexibility. Since they are still frequently trained in the classical tradition, with a strong emphasis on philology, many of these scholars have very often been quite skeptical of the new problematics. Really, these suspicions are often justified, considering how uninformed and even superficial many of the proponents of the new approaches have often been. So zealous are these advocates of a new vision that they frequently belittle, ignore, misunderstand or vilify older contributions and advances, even at times in a rather cavalier manner. Thus, the Orientalists' reaction to all of this is one of understandable irritation and annoyance. Nonetheless, this response, for its part, should not reject the considerable contribution made by a reconsideration of earlier concepts.

These traditionalists are no less suspicious of native specialists. It is true that there are among them many contentious people whose behavior is somewhat exasperating. All European scholarship is dismissed as riddled with a colonial and ethnocentric spirit. At the same time, much or even the essential part of the Orientalists' work is surreptitiously retained by the very people who attack it. What often happens, then, is that the baby is thrown out with the bathwater, at least in the sense of verbal outrage. In reality, however, many indigenous specialists take what they want from European scientific contributions by clothing this data in native garb. Many, too, have not even renounced antiquated methods and outmoded ideologies in their most dogmatic and anti-historical forms. At times, nationalist ideologies allow the opportunistic native specialists to legitimize, in the same breath, their rejection in theory of all that does not suit them in European research and their under-the-table acceptance of whatever furthers their cause or serves its purposes. On extreme occasions, the native specialists have been ill served by the most vocal kinds of opportunists who pose as their spokesmen. These are pure intellectual adventurers skilled in gaining advantage from the anti-colonial sentiments prevailing in international organizations and in large segments of European society. Such representations have met with understandably vigorous opposition from serious Orientalists who regard them as little more than acts of terrorism. The unfortunate results of this are that the serious native scholar is frequently put into the same category as these intellectual adventurers and that many legitimate criticisms of the European contribution to scholarship are not distinguished from slanderous and ignorant ravings.

Finally, traditional Orientalists are quite skeptical of scholars trained in areas peripheral to mainstream nineteenth-century scholarship. Prejudice against these academic disciplines has persisted to the present-day, despite the solid scientific reputations these fields have acquired. Examples of this are the fields of contemporary history and sociology. It is true that there are many academic dilettantes in these two fields, especially since contemporary history and sociology have become the preserve of harried journalists and writers as well as radio and television commentators—many of whom have no real background in either discipline. Indeed, many are impostors and adventurers. Moreover, political militants often use either contemporary history or sociology as the basis for their attacks. Sometimes these assaults are justified, but they are just as often superficial, insulting, and abusive. For traditional Orientalists, a rather conservative group on the whole, such intrusions from outsiders are, to say the least, shocking.

The result of this is that many Orientalists often fall back on traditional and conservative forms of scholarship where they can lead a quiet, industrious existence, working on critical editions of texts, factual history or a "pointillist" style of philology. They quite rightly note the enormous work that remains to be done in all these areas. Theirs is a valid and even indispensable reminder but it does not excuse their often contemptuous attitude toward new disciplines, revised scientific practices or new problematics.

The Present State of the Craft

Here, I will limit myself to my own perception of the major currents and schools of thought. I will mention only a few names since to do more would turn this essay into a sort of honor roll, which would not only be incomplete but very unfair, as I am not acquainted with all the important work currently under way in this vast area.

It should first be pointed out that excluding the major intellectual currents of the United States from the European picture is very misleading. The major trends in European scholarship are, for example, equally prevalent in the United States. Of course, North American scholarship has distinctive characteristics of its own just as does that of Europe. In addition, the sheer size and wealth of the United States means that North America can and does produce more research than Europe.

Naturally, the presentation of what follows will simply be an overview of current trends and schools of thought. All the trends described can be subdivided into numerous smaller currents, each with its own subtle differentiation according to the temperament and background of each scholar.

The Continuance of the Past Impetus

Many works of scholarship, perhaps even the majority, still follow the same patterns as the work of past generations. Nevertheless, the problematics of general humanist sciences have offered modern researchers the opportunity to transcend the past's influence. The following list does not presume in any way to be exhaustive, but it should at least provide a picture of the major areas of research most affected by scientific and technological innovations.

¶ The publication of literary or documentary texts, archival documents, inscriptions, and coins has seen the introduction of new methods, particularly the use of computer technology, quantitative analysis, and coding.

¶ The preparation of reference books, indexes, and catalogues has been enormously influenced by the large-scale application of new methods related to computer science and technology. For example, new techniques are aiding the compilation of the *Onomasticon Arabicum*, a project initiated many years ago and abandoned until rather recently. In addition, without going so far, older reference and research tools are being renewed, corrected, and developed with the help of much more powerful means. For instance, there are the efforts of Sezgin to correct and improve upon Carl Brockelmann's massive work on Arab texts.

¶ Factual history is a discipline toward which, regrettably, the new field of social history is often quite condescending. Fortunately, this is a trend that has not become all-pervasive. Many scholars continue to build on previous work by seeking greater precision in historical detail, verifying details, and determining all the circumstances surrounding historical events. Today, as in the past, distinct styles of scholarship are developing, often the result of individual personalities and also of schools of thought or various trends, even of cyclical swings from extreme criticism of historical sources to blind confidence in them. These factual historians deserve our respect, although there is a tendency among them to believe that general conclusions can easily be reached by foregoing the absolutely essential intermediate step of theoretical analysis. It is only this process that can sift out the causal factors and allot to each its specific rôle. Moreover, erudition is still absolutely necessary in historical research, but despite the arguments of learned scholars, it is not, in itself, sufficient. Of course, there will always be a few imposing scholars who, although they lack a profound knowledge of general problematics, will by their sheer intellect and common sense, produce interesting or fruitful re-readings of texts.

¶ In archaeology, art history, and the aesthetics of Islamic arts there has been much progress. The techniques of excavation and methods of analyzing archaeological findings have become highly sophisticated. Amateur scholars in search of nothing but "beautiful artifacts" and Eurocentrists (or classico-centrists, to coin a new word) with their narrow vision, are rarely encountered now but traces of their influence, which dominated much scholarship until quite recently, can be found to this day. Creative approaches, as illustrated in particular by the work of the French historian, Jean Sauvaget, helped to develop these areas of study in new and productive ways. Scholars are now becoming increasingly aware of the need to establish a kind of global history documented by archaeology, architecture, urbanism, and all kinds of non-literary pieces of information. It is heartening to know that any future history of aesthetics or of taste need no longer be built only on subjective impressions as was the case in past generations (which resulted in the belittling of this type of study) but rather, on a truly solid foundation.

¶ The fields of the history of technology, customs, and mind-sets have made uneven progress. In these areas, indispensable and fruitful specialization has often deteriorated into strictly sealed, compartmentalized disciplines. Unfortunately, the precise, detailed, and extensive information about the Islamic world gathered by these fields has not been sufficiently integrated into either the findings of ethnographers and anthropologists or into scholarship on other cultural areas or even as part of the general problematics. Let us consider for example, how scanty are serious studies devoted to a topic as important as sexuality. There are already several remarkable works of synthesis in all these fields, each with its own virtues and shortcomings.

In this vast area of studies, there is a normal tendency toward what might be called culturalism, a tendency that is associated with the work of the brilliant scholar, Gustave von Grunebaum, among others. According to this notion, culture—variously defined and often reduced to its most salient intellectual or artistic attributes—is understood as an abstract construct of supreme causal efficacy. The historians who subscribe to the school of the history of mindsets at times lean somewhat in this direction. Admittedly, the general perspective prevalent in these disciplines may be found wanting; nevertheless, the research produced has frequently been extremely valuable.

¶ The history of sciences is obviously of great importance. Here, however, there is a rather disturbing shortage of specialists whose expertise extends beyond Near Eastern languages and philological methods to scientific disciplines, such as astronomy, mathematics, and medicine.

¶ The history of institutions has produced too many worthwhile works to be enumerated here. It should, however, be mentioned that critical research based on source materials (as pioneered by Joseph Schacht) as well as the detailed study of jurisprudence, have contributed immensely to an underlying understanding of Muslim law. Jurists trained in Western legal theory but broad-minded enough to consider concepts outside Western law would be extremely welcome.

¶ The study of languages has also been advanced thanks to new factors. With modern methods, it is now considerably easier to collect the necessary data for indispensable research tools such as dictionaries. Moreover, new methods of research in linguistics, first formulated for other areas, such as quantitative and structural analysis or generative grammar, have inspired a complete rethinking of linguistic theory with a more penetrating analysis of structures. At the same time, we should note that the teaching of languages is becoming more effective. Now, specialists are able to learn languages more quickly and more thoroughly so that they are much better equipped to do research. These new methods for teaching languages have also had an impact on theory.

¶ Research in the fields usually brought together under the labels of ethnography, folklore, and anthropology represents more of a renewal than any real development. During the colonial period, these disciplines accumulated a tremendous wealth of information. While most people, including myself, are glad to see an end to colonialism, it is nonetheless undeniable that it is now more difficult than in the past to undertake ethnographic and similar types of scholarly investigations. Nationalist sensitiveness and the suspicions of the newly independent states often make fieldwork an exasperating experience if not simply unfeasible. In addition, modernization destroys older customs and traditions and establishes a kind of modern ideology that denies their reality when they still exist. This predicament is partially offset by refining methods of fieldwork so that the research can often go beyond the simple accumulation of first-hand ethnographic data. In this respect, the excellent studies by Frederik Barth, which are devoted to tribes in Iran, should be mentioned. All the same, it is deplorable that the collection of this type of data, regardless of the method used, is not being pursued more intensely. Much ethnographic information is disappearing before it can be recorded. This is an irreparable loss that should be brought repeatedly to the attention of the young researchers who are more fascinated with theory than with first-hand investigations. It must, however, be remembered that the data collected during the colonial era represents an immensely valuable body of work, even given the faulty ideological orientation of those who haphazardly collected it.

¶ Literary history likewise has benefited from new approaches growing out of advances in linguistics (semiology, and so on). As is often the case, the newcomers to these disciplines tend to exaggerate the importance of their methods while being contemptuous of the valid contributions that have the misfortune of being more conservative. In any event, current work in this field is being carried out by researchers who subscribe to both the old and the new approaches.

¶ Literary history is related to the history of ideas, a field that many persist in reducing to the history of theology. Nonetheless, the publication and translation of texts now under way have resulted in monographs devoted either to individual writers, to specific periods or to intellectual currents, all of which can be extremely useful.

Theologocentrism in Scholarship

Those schools of thought that believe that almost all observable phenomena can be explained by reference to Islam, in societies where Muslims are the majority or where Islam in the official religion, suffer from what I will call theologocentrism. In the past, such a vision was held implicitly by all researchers in the field. However, when positivism was at its height, a number of writers worked against the theologocentric influence in their scientific work, even though they did not explicitly reject it and may not even have been aware that their work contradicted it. Today, this theologocentric vision is more often openly disputed, its validity at least is rather frequently questioned. Nonetheless, present tendencies toward irrationalism, or at least toward challenging confident rationalist assertions of the past, favor the theologocentric vision. Fewer scholars and even less of the educated public subscribe to those notions that are the foundation of the theologocentric position. However, identifiable segments of the academic-intellectual world and quasi-scholarly circles steeped in irrationalism and even many laymen are now more articulate and sophisticated in their defense of theologocentrism. Parenthetically and contrary to what many academic specialists undoubtedly think, in a history devoted to the evolution of ideas or in a structural study of common ideologies, it is impossible to strictly separate the scholars from the laymen. Despite claims to the contrary, every intellectual world is permeated with the ideas of the society in which it operates. On the other hand, some of the conclusions reached by scholars eventually find their way into the thinking of the general public, often losing much along the way. Therefore, at times, proponents of theologocentrism are given to aggressive assertions of its superiority, claiming it has the capacity to give direction to the entire field. In the past, such pretentions went unchallenged and therefore barely expressed, unlike today when they are forced into rigorous theoretical debate or pushed to logical limits.

Let us consider the major trends derived from or related to this school of thought. Several tendencies can be discerned.

¶ The sympathetic, but nevertheless distant and discreetly critical, study of Muslim theology is being conducted by European scholars of different spiritual inclinations, including Christians adhering to Thomistic rationalism such as Louis Gardet and M. M. Anawati. Given their education and specializations, these scholars naturally have a predilection for the theologocentric vision. This is stronger insofar as their own existential orientation is itself slanted toward the predominance of a religious or even mystical spirituality. Nevertheless, much of their analyses and conclusions could be accepted by those of completely different persuasions. The aspect of their work most open to criticism is their occasional attempts at extending their problematic to areas outside the strictly religious.

¶ Muslim apologetics, which will not be considered here, naturally flourishes in the Islamic world, and Europe is more indulgent of it than ever. There is a large, or at least, vocal anti-colonial, anti-ethnocentric sentiment now evident in Europe. This, combined with the Christian ecumenical movement, which seeks to make amends for past wrongs committed against Muslims, has resulted in the notion that any criticism of Islamic dogma, ritual or even of the traditional practices of Muslim societies, is a remnant of the older, imperialistic, colonial attitudes. A general retreat from positivism has accentuated this phenomenon. The conclusions of Orientalists of past generations regarding the writing of Muslim "sacred history" and the composition of the Qur'ān are now being questioned. Until recently, these critical conclusions were accepted as relatively definitive scientific findings (and so they are to my mind).

¶ A special place should be made for the Orientalist successors of Louis Massignon's brand of mystical spiritualism sympathetic to Islam. Massignon developed his style of scholarship during the height of the positivist era as a reaction against the dominant tendencies of that period. It should be remembered that Massignon was a scholar tormented by contradictions yet endowed with immense erudition and incisive intellect. He relied on what he called a personal "mental litmus test," which was his own analytical device for understanding intellectual attitudes from the Islamic past. New tendencies (see below) that go beyond the analytical methods prevalent during the positivist era have reinforced the influence of this style of scholarship. The metahistorical method of Henry Corbin represents the extreme example of this approach. Corbin, who knew much about Iranian mystical philosophy in the Muslim period, applied a phenomenological approach to draw certain conclusions, which all advocates of this approach would probably not consider as inevitably resulting from it. Corbin's assertions were of great theoretical clarity and aggressiveness on the absolute necessity, to his mind, of disregarding history and social conditioning. He arrived at an idealized reconstruction of the history of Muslim philosophy. His reconstruction is fatally flawed because it revolves around Shī'ite thinking as it was expressed in a late period, while Corbin transfers these ideas to more ancient stages, presuming an immutability of the doctrine, against common sense and the opinion of most scholars. Less erudite and more pragmatic is the extreme wing of esotericism as seen in the works of F. Schuon and T. Burckhardt, who followed the lead of René Guénon. Nevertheless, the works of these authors are not without valid insights, even for those who do not share their existential convictions. The most extreme act for the scholar of Muslim theology is conversion to Islam, pure and simple: René Guénon did just that.

¶ The introduction of new problematics in the studies and analyses of the psychism of the soul of the religious experience and its exterior manifestations has been fruitful. Sometimes, this will happen within the theologocentric sphere; sometimes it will occur outside that sphere or it may even oscillate, not very intelligibly, between opposing spheres. Alluded to here is the work of Waardenburg in phenomenology, T. Izutsu, M. Arkoun, and others in the semiology of religious discourse as well as the diverse uses of structuralist methodologies.

New Fields and Disciplines

New disciplines have been created, further elaborated or endowed with a certain scientific legitimacy. The older disciplines have been adapted to new areas and fields of inquiry. Let us point out briefly the considerable, but still inadequate, advances in the study of the more recent historical eras that have been prejoratively called periods of decline: Iran in the post-Mongol period, the Ottoman Empire, and so on. Admittedly, Europe's preoccupation with the immense power of the Ottoman state contributed to its intense and sophisticated study in the past. And, although there has recently been a flurry of interest in the Ottoman Empire, scholarship on the subject is perhaps still inferior to previous levels. In addition, the history of contemporary movements and states is generally held in higher regard than in the past. These fields have made significant progress, particularly after Claude Cahen defended economic and social history in 1955. The first conference devoted entirely to this area took place in London in 1967.

The study of the sociology of Islam is not really a new field. Proof of its long history is furnished by the overly ambitious work of Reuben Levy published in the 1930s.[4] Any work that is not purely concerned with events falls within the realm of the sociological, at least in one of the commonly accepted meanings of the word. Every year, in the first decades of the twentieth century, Durkheim's *Année sociologique* reviewed a few books on the Islamic world past and present. Louis Massignon, who contributed somewhat later to these reviews, called his course at the Collège de France "Sociography of the Muslim World." In fact, it is in this sense of sociographic studies that most current work can be classified. C. A. O. van Nieuwenhuijze has published a synthesis of this kind of work that even goes beyond it.[5] Yet, studies that are purely and exclusively sociological (for example, some by the latter author) have only been published in recent years. I mean a type of scholarship that goes further than the very useful but simple description of attitudes in order to infer from the Islamic phenomena conclusions on a level with contributions to the general theory of society or, which, at least, could within theoretical visions of this kind.

While a number of works have been published in other new disciplines that are either partially or wholly based on data drawn from the Muslim world, I will limit myself to a discussion of those mentioned above. For the moment, let me simply state that in many areas and for many thinkers, there is an urgent need to overcome the traditional isolationism of Islamic studies.

Regional Influences in Islamic Studies

As was briefly noted above, the various countries of Europe (and America) display at least a superficially wide range of trends in scholarship. This situation is brought about by several factors: the degree of influence the latest intellectual currents have had on a country; the degree of receptiveness permitted by the national academic system; and the extent to which the traditional Orientalist etablishment was either isolated from or linked to other sections of this system. The history of Oriental studies in each country is a major factor in their current status.

A vastly illuminating work would be a country-by-country survey that would not restrict itself to a dry enumeration of published works, but instead, would delve into the underlying reasons for the various intellectual trends prevalent in each of these countries. Obviously, this is an impossible task for me here. I will, therefore, refer the reader for a sample of what I mean to a work by C. A. O. van Nieuwenhuijze that attempts to do this sort of study for the Netherlands.[6]

I will, however, provide an overview of certain large-scale trends in the growth of Islamic Orientalism in the "socialist" countries of Eastern Europe. It should be pointed out that this evolution, which in an earlier period was remarkable, indeed, audacious, is now mostly restricted to the type of detailed studies associated with traditional Orientalism. The reasons for this are not difficult to understand. With the university hierarchy, it is dangerous (and at times impossible), at least as far as personal advancement is concerned, to suggest even slightly original ideas. In so doing, one risks going against official doctrines and arousing the hostility of the intellectual class (more or less competent) upon whom the state and the party have conferred the exclusive right of elaborating theory. This does not mean, however, that such theory is without valid elements nor does it mean that all original ideas that are rejected are actually worthwhile.

It is only by taking into consideration the situation in Eastern Europe that the advantages and the difficulties of the freedom of expression can be understood. When confronted with the mass of more or less inept works appearing daily in the West, about the only solace one can find in it all is that, bad and even dangerous as it might be, it does represent freedom of expression. Given the intellectual climate in Eastern Europe, it is easy to understand why researchers have retreated into the scholarly areas of: empirical and detailed works, often of excellent quality; extremely meticulous editions of texts; the compilation of carefully conceived dictionaries frequently containing numerous and valuable ethnographic, historical, and literary materials, such as the dictionaries of the Turkic languages published in the Soviet Union.

All of this obviously does not hinder the underground development of new ideas that will eventually rise to the surface. They can occasionally be discerned in certain publications, though generally clothed in the ritualistic formulas of official doctrine. Thus, references to classical Marxist books contained in much of this scholarship must be considered intellectual camouflage. For a situation similar to this in the West, one has only to remember the conditions surrounding intellectual endeavors during the periods of absolute monarchy or when the state and the Church in alliance imposed their ideology. It is gratifying to recall that even under these circumstances, which were hardly inviting from our present viewpoint, progress was achieved in scholarship, at least during favorable periods.

Paradoxically, it should also be noted that the regimes of Eastern Europe often permit a certain degree of freedom to religious apologetics, although only in restricted fields. The expression of ideas theoretically contrary to the state's official ideology is permitted as long as these ideas are not widely disseminated to the public. The public does not totally adhere to the official ideology anyway. This is true only for areas that do not have an immediate impact on anything actually connected to the functioning of the regime. Moreover, such scholarship hardly poses a threat to these regimes since it plays the rôle of a kind of social safety valve, which ultimately benefits the state. Thus, one sees the flowering of extremely traditional Catholic apologetics in Poland, and the most narrow type of Muslim dogmatism in Yugoslavia.

The Modalities of Future Progress

What is the future for studies devoted to the Muslim world? Which directions and attitudes represent the most rewarding avenues of research? In what follows, I will offer my personal opinions, which are, of course, relative and partly subjective.

It is not desirable to reject or abandon the extensive and valuable accumulation of knowledge from the past two centuries. This body of data is an infinitely rich corpus of material, which could be, of course, partially or wholly re-

considered. But, the disappearance of this material would
be an incalculable cultural loss for all our societies. Not
only would the rejection of it be a tragedy, it would also
be catastrophic to abandon the values of scientific purism
that prevailed in the past.

It has always been true that a researcher must constantly struggle to reach objective interpretations, even if,
logically speaking, the goal of pure objectivity is unattain-
able. Some have suggested that since this ideal is beyond
our reach, it can justifiably be ignored. Instead, they consciously and voluntarily subject their research to the dogmas of certain ideological positions (even if these are, at
best, deserving), which is tantamount to jumping out of
the frying pan into the fire. There is an abundance of
examples from the past that show how disastrous the consequences of this can be.

Scholars must be sensitive to the many indispensable
detours and the distance that must be achieved before research can be formed into solid theories. As Marx once
observed: "There are no royal avenues for science." Slow
but methodical advance is what characterizes the scientific
method. Great leaps forward are authorized very rarely,
and then only after the conclusions attained have been
checked and rechecked to verify the new path. The scholar
must always bear in mind the first of the aphorisms of Hippocrates: "Life is short, art is long, opportunity is easily
lost, empiricism is dangerous, to reason is difficult."[7] This
motto, which is the foundation of Western science, was
translated into Arabic and became a favorite of Muslim
scholars.

The scientific approach should also encompass areas
that in the past were only of minor significance. Of necessity, the scientific method pushes research toward the
theoretical or at least prepares the way for the elaboration
of theory. Any attempt at theoretical elaboration must

now take into account the most recent general problematics. Nonetheless, theoretical elaboration should be accomplished without being slavish to these problematics. Nor should one ascribe to them any more than what they are, namely, conclusions and constructs that are the tentative and provisional results of syntheses reflecting a given historical period and containing much that is largely speculative. Moreover, it is absolutely essential that scientific collaboration between Western and indigenous scholars be organized and that their scholarship be integrated, no matter what difficulties that may present (see above).

Of equal importance is the process of bringing into the mainstream of Islamic studies those topics that were once scorned or considered of only marginal importance. Examples of these are the study of non-classical periods (mistakenly called "decadent") and non-factual history, such as the study of attitudes and customs.

It is also necessary to go beyond the simple collection of data. The act of collecting data is always conditioned by the preconceived notions and unconscious ideas imparted to the scholar by his own social milieu and individual background. Beyond this process of data collection should lie the goals of the formulation of problems. These problems must be posed within the kind of framework that will give them meaning. This is to my mind the sociological or anthropological approach.

Also needed is a concerted effort to integrate current events and developments into the mainstream of Islamic studies. It is not worthwhile to attempt to link these events to a pure and simple continuation of classical Islamic civilization. Rather, they should be studied within the framework of a contemporary global history, sociology, and anthropology. This means that the researcher must try to understand the contemporary intellectual trends and problems in that society. But this does not mean to follow slavishly its current fads, trends or ideologies. Western scholars of the Islamic world must not forget that they are rooted in a different milieu. Rather, they can advance research about other cultural worlds by bringing to the self-examination going on in other societies the contribution of the lessons drawn from the workings of this milieu itself or from their possible knowledge of wider areas. What I am advocating here is the need to carefully examine the way a given people or society views its own problems, which does not mean one should embrace it wholly or uncritically. Their perspective is of paramount importance. How they see things should be analyzed, its origins should be appreciated, and its valid elements revealed to the enrichment of the scholar's scientific approach. This dialectical process will benefit both the society studied and the society that studies it.

Admittedly, many enormous obstacles stand in the way of the realization of this ideal program. Certainly, such a program will meet with misunderstanding or suspicion, often of an extremely disagreeable sort. But, if science is to progress, this price must be paid. In the long run, seriousness and intellectual honesty in research are recognized. By remaining faithful to the principles of the scientific method, even the most vilified of researchers will find supporters of his ideas who follow the same path. The scholar of principles sows the seeds for ideas that will one day come to fruition. At the same time, his own thought will grow richer.

Science exists and will continue as long as humanity survives. Science appears to be fundamental to human societies, all of which engage in some sort of scientific activity. These scientific practices always fall into the same categories. It is absurd to reject entirely one or another of them, as is sometimes proposed by ideologue-intellectuals who brand the practice of them as stained by impure motivations. Those scientific tasks laid out at the beginning of this chapter must be and will be pursued, no matter what future guises they assume.

Proposals for Future Study

In rereading the preceding pages, I suddenly have some misgivings about the overall impression they will make on the reader. It seems to me that I have been overly optimistic. The reason for this is clear: I was writing for and addressing scholars who do not need my lessons. I saw positive trends in their work, and placed confidence in them with the hope that these trends will continue and will ultimately succeed in dispelling any negative influences that still affect Oriental studies. Positive currents certainly exist and will be reinforced for the most part by the entry of young researchers into the field. Nonetheless, the overall state of affairs leaves less room for optimism than it might seem.

An accusing finger is usually pointed at the legacy of the past and at all the failings of ideology that inspired colonialism. Such accusations can be justified at least in part. But, too often it is assumed that decolonization has already eliminated or will soon eliminate all these faults or that a radical anti-colonialist (and even anti-neocolonialist) attitude will protect against their recurrence.

In my estimation, such notions are completely mistaken. It is not simply a matter of past legacies, for in fact, the present greatly influences our thought. This needs to be emphasized. Western specialists who study the diverse countries, peoples, societies, and civilizations of the Muslim East (or elsewhere) are themselves not only part of their own collectively privileged societies but often they come from the upper strata of those societies. Overrated conclusions should not be drawn from this fact, nonetheless, it should not be forgotten that social origins will have an influence on scholarship. This quite normal and undeniable situation can lead to distortions in scholarly thinking and points of view. Modern intellectuals would laugh at anyone who pretended otherwise. The result has been that many have decided they can surrender to their favorite ideology since subjectivity will permeate their scholarship anyway.

Those who use such excuses might be defended if they did not always seem to be engaging in behavior quite opposed to that which they purport to believe. While on one hand, they completely reject the idea of objectivity, on the other hand, they are continually resorting to polemics to prove their points. In so doing, they unconsciously admit the contrary. To maintain that their conception of things is superior, more admissible or more coherent means nothing, if not that it is more in agreement with some real, objective quality of these things. If I say there is no truth, how could I argue that this very statement is true?

Consequently, let me say here that the intellectual conditioning in question is not a hopeless evil. What has been said regarding the Middle Ages would appear to confirm this. But, neither should it be imagined that there is an easy remedy for our dilemmas: for example, in the issue confronting us, by replacing our past prejudices against peoples who have been or are currently dominated by other societies by an absolute adherence to all the conceptions of the latter. To heterogeneous currents of thought, there are no universally triumphant alternatives or magical solutions, both of which constitute the fatal illusions of all Stalinisms. Nothing is so simple; contradictions are often insoluble, and we must learn to live with them.

Let me attempt to summarize my observations and form them into some proposals to advance future study.

¶ There is, in fact, no such thing as Orientalism, Sinology, Iranology, and so forth. Rather, there are scientific disciplines defined both by the object of their study and by the direction that study takes, such as sociology, demography, political economy, linguistics, anthropology, ethnology or the various branches of general history. These disciplines can be used to study peoples or regions in a given historical period and still take into account the specificities of those peoples or regions at a particular moment in time.

¶ There is no such thing as the East. In reality, there are simply large numbers of peoples, countries, regions, societies, and cultures that exist in our world. Some of these share similar features that are either of a temporary or permanent quality. Every study devoted to one or several of these entities taken together must justify itself by reference to commonly shared characteristics prevalent in a specific historical period. Other traits that are specific to only one of these units should be left outside these clusters and studied apart.

¶ There are still Orientalists who are imprisoned, many quite contentedly, in their own small cells of Orientalism. The concept of Orientalism itself sprang from pragmatic necessities that forced themselves on European scholars devoted to the study of other cultures. This situation was reinforced by European dominance over other societies, and the result was a greatly distorted vision of things.

¶ The demands of specialization and the desire for career advancement—both all-pervasive elements—have contributed to the Orientalists' self-satisfied acceptance of their academic ghetto. While specialization is obligatory to the conducting of serious and profound scientific work, it tends at the same time to promote a narrow and restricted vision. Concentrating on an academic career and on the interests of the profession is replete with attractions and dangers: the gratification obtained from recognition, the prestige of earning honors and degrees (not without personal material advantages), the excitement of struggles for power—power the scope of which is wretchedly limited but the possession of which arouses passions worthy of a Ceasar or a Napoleon! It is probably inevitable that self-interested career advancement increases the distortions already caused by specialization. A surgeon who saves one's life also has his professional failings, but his skill is appreciated nonetheless. It should be noted that the developing countries can ill-afford intellectual specialists and must pay dearly for that since intellectual dilettantes are usually worse!

The isolation of Orientalist scholars is often aggravated by specialists in other fields who are reluctant to move into areas they do not know well, although they could have provided interesting contributions (notwithstanding some minor inadequacies, perhaps) to infringe on another colleague's intellectual territory. Their caution is commendable but with this sort of reasoning, no one gains.

Marx characterized as "parliamentary cretinism" the tendency to view life only through the prism of parliamentary struggles. Idiots of this type are legion. To conceive of scientific problems exclusively within the limits of one's speciality and to test them only with the usual practices of one's discipline is a form of cretinism that persists to this very day. The situation offers huge psychological advantage for the scholar who can stake out areas of research for himself and his colleagues that can be monopolized by sovereign academic rulers, fending off outside interference no matter how beneficial it might be. In all fairness, however, it must be said that the work of dedicated specialists is usually so demanding that to go beyond it—aside from tinkering here and there with a few miscellaneous ideas—is rarely accomplished and then only through an immense effort. Despite these difficulties, scholarly work, even that restricted to erudition for its own sake, moving ceaselessly and amassing myriad invaluable findings along the way.

¶ The negative aspects of these attitudes are aggravated by the many who follow a conformist brand of conservatism. This philosophy stems from social origins and circumstances, even if it is not the inevitable consequence. The same class background can produce conservatives as well as revolutionaries. And, the farther the revolutionaries are removed from the concrete situation, the greater will be their extremism.

On the other hand, conservatism is often a visceral condition. Conformism is simply the surface coating of a conservative state of mind that believes being unfaithful to established structures is a mistake bordering on scandal. Ideas are dismissed not because they are considered mistaken, but because they are unbecoming. It is true that advanced capitalist societies, with their mechanisms for self-perpetuation, often honor and reward dissidents. Yet, their traditional structures remain firmly entrenched and conservative reactions are a frequent phenomena. Simply stated, often there are pragmatic reasons for staying within the norm or for returning to that norm after a small deviation, an act that in itself may confer honor. On the whole, one has more chances of "success" and of social and professional mobility by acting within the established structures.

Conservatism dreads, distrusts, and fears change. All destabilization (now a very popular term with its prejorative meaning) is disquieting. It is rejected and denied wherever possible by minimizing its influence, its reality or its depth. However, it is actually destabilization that is the law of history. It is simply part of the cycle.

Conservatives will de-emphasize change, preferring instead to make present social structures appear timeless. These structures become the essence of all things, and the conservative becomes fundamentally an essentialist.

In this sort of thinking, modern relationships cannot be considered in a state of flux because they have been tied to timeless essences. There are an infinite variety of essentialisms: for races, peoples, ideology, even for classes and the state. Paradoxically, essentialism can even be made to advocate revolts and revolution if such upheavals quickly lead to a restabilization that will be advantageous to the essentialists.

To put one essence at the top not only neglects the structures that make up that essence but also those that will undermine that essence, leading ultimately to its destruction. This amounts to reducing it to a pure, unconditioned idea. It is a form of idealism. No one knows with any certainty what historical materialism means. Only one definition is valid: the struggle against historical idealism, itself a polymorphous, tangible, and spontaneous hydra that is always ready to re-emerge. Historical idealism is even occasionally produced by some of our philosophers who presume to be materialists.

The conservative majority not only refuses to grant legitimacy to today's revolts, but even tries to deny their existence. They justify their attitude by harping on the rebels' misdeeds and revolutionary language, which will, in all likelihood, contain many errors and proposterous notions. But all of this ridiculous phraselogy and even their repulsive actions will not negate the fact that these people have good cause for complaint and rebellion. Nevertheless, it is necessary to know how to see beyond all of this without either excusing the process of mystification, conservative or revolutionary, or being oblivious to those reprehensible practices, which conservatives have only partially and recently abandoned.

¶ Conservatism forces the conservative to shrink from any ideas, notions or practices that appear to be connected to destabilization. Certainly, the ideas advanced by racist essentialism remain largely discredited, at least when such a position is publicly admitted. However, traces of this brand of essentialism persist and racist attitudes have not been eliminated simply because decolonization has occurred. True, the majority of moderate Orientalists no longer accept the theologocentric vision with the serene assurance of the past. Nonetheless, here too it is easy to slip back into practices that one renounces in theory. The success of political movements under the guise of religion can only encourage a resurgence of essentialism.

At least superficially, racism and some other brands of essentialism have been rejected and no longer cause much discussion. However, the same cannot be said for any idea that seems to have, even remotely, certain similarities to Marxist problematics. Such ideas, even when mentioned in passing, could cause all sorts of consternation. This explains, I believe, the revulsion of many for any over-arching analysis based on social mechanisms. This is particularly true when ideological factors are given a derivative status, making them largely a consequence of other conditioning factors. (It should be remembered that the term *derivation* is from Pareto and not from Marx.) All those who are inclined to consider economic, political or social forces of foremost importance, even when this prominence is restricted to a given level or aspect, present the conservative with the truly frightening specter of the Gulag and the threat of popular revolts in the developing world. The strategic, partial alliance between the so-called socialist states and revolutionary leaders of the Third World only reinforce the conservatives' fears, just as do the authoritarian practices of governments in newly independent nations.

Political attitudes, even disguised as apoliticalism, compel global and historical visions. Out of the conservatives' own fear and loathing comes the refusal to see society in a structured totality. What results is a hodgepodge of explanations, all of which seek a perfect, but illusory, setting in the face of competing explanatory systems. It is, of course, a hopeless quest.

There are certain advantages to invoking a multitude of disparate factors, whose very disorder (if even admitted) is considered a natural state of affairs. The intellectual, essentially motivated by his search for success, can delude himself and his audience into thinking he has been successful with shimmering canvases of infinite variety. All of these give the impression of encountering multiform reality, of obtaining an utter freedom of the mind, and the liberty to pay tribute to the myriad facets of the world's diverse ethnic or national cultures.

If many are attracted to the new problematics, they are confronted by a variety of options, which become, in fact, intellectual refuges. They can pretend to throw themselves into truly new and innovative structuralist techniques but they are only innovative in a limited way: in linguistics, in the theory of literature or partly in anthropological analyses, and so on. Similarly, the field of global, non-factual history encompassing the long range, and of the history of mind-sets are areas in which scholars can dabble. Other examples of this kind of special, passionate, and exclusive devotion could be cited in the areas of psychoanalysis and of mathematics applied to new fields. The admittedly very important rôle of language in human behavior and social relations has often been and still is overemphasized, but this has produced some very fascinating studies.

All of these approaches have their enthusiasts. However, the main criticism is that each of these approaches believes it has a monopoly on the truth. Those committed to the new approaches believe they are participating in a revolutionary undertaking that will mature and evolve, encompassing ever greater numbers of researchers until the accepted notions are completely overturned. This results

in an exclusive and often fanatical enthusiasm. What these
devotees fail to realize is that the revolution is only partial,
that it does not always shake global conceptions, and even
that it tends to dissuade them from efforts to attain a
global view of society. In particular, in these approaches,
they find innumerable ways to avoid the central issue of
supreme power (I mean here the power in a society or political power, not the many forms of diffuse power) and of
the social situation, which permits either the exercise of
power or assaults on it. Thus, to omit this dimension of
prime importance is to risk misunderstanding the underlying mechanisms of a society. Such an omission misun-
derstands the whole fabric of society and its workings, it
ignores or plays down the fundamental drive of all societies
to assure their own survival and reproduction.

Conservatives, except the most narrow-minded sort,
are indulgent of innovative approaches. But, the conservatives object to all conceptualizations that grant a key
rôle to economic, political or social forces. Aside from ob-
jections of a political nature alluded to above, they ac-
cuse those who subscribe to such thinking of reductionism.
They seem to believe that by conferring on one of many
factors a certain relative weight in explanatory schemes,
everything else will be reduced in-relation to it! But no-
body ever clearly denounces the current real reductionism,
expressed or masked, of all factors to the sole ideological
(ordinary religious) factor.

Even when conservative Orientalists are willing to admit the fundamental importance to our times of popular
revolts arising from political or social domination, struggles between social actors from different backgrounds, in
short, from the nature of social relationships, they would
prefer to confine social upheaval to the twentieth century,
or at most to the nineteenth century. Attempts to detect
these same factors at work in a more distant past are met

with distress and disgust or at least uneasiness. This attitude results in an explicit refusal to recognize permanent or recurring structures in history. Present-day events and even terminology, when applied to the past, assume in their view an obscene character, so to speak. They justify their positions by historicism, more precisely, by a stated desire not to project the conditions of the present onto the past.

Such a refusal is legitimate and even beneficial in combatting the anachronisms unleashed by past and present ideologues. Yet, such a refusal should not be allowed to go beyond certain limits. One would not go so far as to echo the saying of the fourteenth-century Arab sociologist of genius, Ibn Khaldun, who wrote: "The future resembles the past more than water resembles water." Nonetheless, his words contain a germ of sociological truth regarding the persistence of permanent or recurring structures over time, place, and social formation. This is true simply because there are laws that apply to every possible kind of human society as well as to all societies of the same type.

¶ Most scholars in the disciplines with which we are concerned resolve their intellectual predicament by following, without questioning, the precedents established by their predecessors and by pursuing the pure work of erudite accumulation. At times, however, they are motivated by the desire to make some startling discovery and they think they can make science advance by formulating an extraordinary theory, by combining known elements in a novel way or by refuting accepted dates, places or facts. Or, they elevate to the level of general theory a finding drawn from some narrow sphere. The result is rarely positive and, more often than not, quite pathetic.

In any case, such specialists fail to see that they are influenced, even in their choice of subject matter, by implicit ideas—those of their historical era, of their social rank, and of their teachers. These ideas weigh heavily on many of their conclusions and even on details, on the few questions they ask themselves, and on the numerous questions they fail to ask. These implicit ideas channel research in a certain direction and not another. It is not a simple matter to intellectually escape from one's own society and environment.

¶ We must remember not to overlook remarkable accomplishments because their authors' underlying ideas (implicit or explicit) are debatable. Of little merit were the notions held by the French Egyptologist Jean François Champollion (1790–1832) concerning society; after all, his brilliance was in deciphering hieroglyphics! This has been sufficiently developed above so that I may limit myself here to merely mentioning it is passing. What is absolutely necessary is to steadfastly resist all new attempts at Zhdanovism, which tomorrow may come from the right in our countries, but, which at the moment, are most forcefully advocated by the extreme left and the totalitarian regimes of whatever persuasion in newly independent countries.

I have discussed above the dangers inherent in the theory of two sciences toward which all challenge to authority normally tend. One is alway tempted to discredit all the enemy has said, is saying, and will say, as fatally flawed by his essentially evil nature (how could an enemy be good?) or by the spurious basis of his ideas, and to apply this rejection even to scientific matters. From this arises the conclusion that only people on our side are capable of producing valuable knowledge. This theory, like many of the same genre, is the distorted reflection of observations and ideas similar to those that I have just formulated and which seem to me to be solidly based. The effects of the application of this theory can only be catastrophic. It is quite true that all scientific work and all research is tied to the general conceptualizations permeating either the dominant classes or those in opposition within a society. But such links are rarely immediate and the relationship with the political orientations of these classes is more often contradictory and indirect. It is also true that all scientific conclusions have repercussions, although sometimes infinitesimal, upon the structures and options of the society in which they are formulated. But, in most cases, these repercussions are indirect, complex, and contradictory.

In totalitarian regimes of the so-called right or left, the notion of the origins and consequences of scientific work motivate the total mobilization of scholars in the service of an ideological line that coincides with governmental policies. This is equally true of political parties that are highly organized and disciplined with a rigorous ideological indoctrination. At work here is nothing as benign as the diffuse influences of class or social background; rather, what is in question are the imperial edicts of an irresponsible bureaucratic center that is generally incompetent as well. What can stand in opposition to this dangerous mobilization, which is so fatal to science and frequently even to those interests that it was meant to defend? It is, quite simply put, the relative but real autonomy of research and the freedom, so vital for researchers, if any results are to be expected from their work. Except during the most repressive periods, this is a principle that has been defended, at least with regard to those studies that have the fewest ties to prevailing ideologies. Generally speaking, areas or zones for free work can be found; these zones can be preserved even in those whom devotion to a higher and common cause excites self-denial. At work within humanity and observable everywhere, is an irrepressible drive toward autonomy in the achievement of tasks. As has already been discussed, excessive specialization as well as the arduousness of scholarly research can limit and distort viewpoints. On the other hand, when tyrannies attempt to mobilize all society to their own purposes, such specializations and research can provide safe havens and refuges—zones of liberty that are preserved for a future when freer scientific activity can eventually be disseminated, as was seen above.

¶ Orientalism and its distorted ideologies constitute but one example of scientific activity gone astray. There are no miraculous cures or panaceas for the errors, contradictions, blind alleys, and aporias inherent in scientific activity. The antidote for the Orientalists' involvement in the dominant ideologies of liberal, bourgeois society, is not to blindly adopt opposing ideologies, however tempting such a course of action might be.

Nor is the remedy to be found in the vulgarized, dogmatized, and ideologized Marxism of either Marxist institutions, states or counter states. While the criticism coming from this direction is often on the mark and healthy, since its theories encompass certain valid elements, to steer in this direction leads to myths no less illusory and destructive than those that Marxism quite rightfully attacks. Essentialism and idealism as applied to races, nations or peoples are reappearing in new disguises in states proclaiming to be inspired by Marxism. Idealist essentialism brings disastrous results when applied to a particular social class (often a fictitious one at that) or to the so-called socialist state, which regards itself as inherently above error.

Neither is the cure found in the nationalist ideologies of dependent or formerly colonized states, no matter how genuine their complaints, how pertinent their criticisms or how necessary taking all this into account seems to be. However, these criticisms are frequently too abbreviated, for criticism that is confined to the nationalist level generally tends to replace the apologetics of a nation or a group of nations with that of another nation or group. From a scientific point of view, this does not lead very far. The consequences wrought by intellectual terrorism and militant conformism more often serve the interests of Third World intellectuals and bureaucrats—themselves a privileged class—than the masses they claim to represent. This does not diminish the relevance of their observations but these, too, are not exempt from critical examination and should not be passively or submissively accepted. As an example, on a favorite theme of Third World intellectuals (but where their criticism is often misdirected), studies undertaken of a particular society by those outside it may well be wrong in orientation and malicious. Yet, in and of itself, this is not a crime, rather it is a right that must be safeguarded and a immensely useful contribution that is indispensable to a total understanding of the self.

¶ Studies devoted to the peoples, cultures, and societies of the numerous regions previously grouped under the rubric of the East will continue. Henceforth, specialists from the countries under study will participate in growing numbers in this research. Neither indigenous nor Western scholars can be miraculously spared the hurdles that ideologies and social conditioning throw in front of their perception of things—whether it is a question of factors emanating from a particular historical juncture or those constraints that are inherent to all intellectual activity throughout the ages.

A certain progress will be realized even if it is only the effect of accumulated knowledge. Nevertheless, radical measures that attempt to spare researchers from the obstacles that impede their efforts simply do not work. Understanding can only be advanced in the very midst of constraints and contradictions, and these are similar or even identical to those that operated in the past. Theoretical advances are neither made spontaneously from the facts, nor through the application of a single, great idea inspired by a flash of genius, nor by theorizations that neglect a global vision of society, nor from the study of one limited domain.

¶ Scholarly studies exert a great deal less influence on the ideas current in a given society than the latter exert on intellectual milieus. The perceptions held regarding a counterpart of another culture are less concerned with the reality than whether that counterpart appears to be a threat or a hope, whether it is somehow related to the observer's passions or interests or can reinforce or illustrate internal trends and currents in the observer society. Foreign peoples or cultural universes are loved or hated, not as the result of loose passions, but for reasons rooted in the observer's own society. The images held pass through the usual prism of ideological formation and evolution. This process represents a vast field of inquiry whose study has scarcely begun.

Notes

Introduction

1. *The Legacy of Islam*, 2d ed., edited by Joseph Schacht with C. E. Bosworth (Oxford: Oxford University Press, 1974). My paper, entitled "The Western Image and Western Studies of Islam," appears on pages 9–62. The first edition of *The Legacy of Islam* was published by Oxford University Press in 1931 and was edited by Sir Thomas Arnold and Alfred Guillaume.

3. Many details can be found in the very erudite book of Father Youakim Moubarac, *Recherches sur la pensée chrétienne et l'Islam dans les temps modernes et à l'époque contemporaine* (Beirut, 1977). His synthetic views are slanted by his concern for a dialogue between the faithful of Islam and Christendom. This is not something I care to concern myself with. The Tunisian historian and essayist Hichem Djait wrote an insightful work on the topic entitled *L'Europe et l'Islam* (Paris, 1978). The book is very valuable for his often brilliant and sensitive ideas, with which I agree in the main. He focused his attention, more than I do here, on certain points and authors. Edward Said's *Orientalism* (New York, 1978) had a great and unexpected success. There are many valuable ideas in it. Its great merit, to my mind, was to shake the self-satisfaction of many Orientalists, to appeal to them (with questionable success) to consider the sources and the connections of their ideas, to cease to see them as a natural, unprejudiced conclusion of the facts, studied without any presup-

position. But, as usual, his militant stand leads him repeatedly to make excessive statements. This problem is accentuated because as a specialist of English and comparative literature, he is inadequately versed in the practical work of the Orientalists. It is too easy to choose, as he does, only English and French Orientalists as a target. By so doing, he takes aim only at representatives of huge colonial empires. But there was an Orientalism before the empires, and the pioneers of Orientalism were often subjects of other European countries, some without colonies. Much too often, Said falls into the same traps that we old Communist intellectuals fell into some forty years ago, as I will explain below. The growth of Orientalism was linked to the colonial expansion of Europe in a much more subtle and intricate way than he imagines. Moreover, his nationalistic tendencies have prevented him from considering, among others, the studies of Chinese or Indian civilization, which are ordinarily regarded as part of the field of Orientalism. For him, the Orient is restricted to *his* East, that is, the Middle East. Muslim countries outside the Arab world (after all, four Muslims in five are not Arabs), and even Arab nations in the West receive less than their due in his interpretation.

Western Views of the Muslim World

1. J. M. Wallace-Hadrill, ed. and trans., *Fredegarii Chronicon: The Fourth Book of the Chronicle of Fredegar, with Its Continuations* (London, 1960), sec. 66, pp. 54–55.
2. Wallace-Hadrill, *Fredegarii Chronicon*, sec. 81, pp. 68–69.
3. B. Colgrave, and R. Mynors, eds. and trans., *Bede's Ecclesiastical History of the English People* (Oxford, 1969), bk. 5, chap. 23, pp. 556–57.
4. F. Kurze, ed. *Annales regni Francorum* in *Scriptores rerum Germanicarum in usum scholarum* (Hanover, 1895), pp. 94–95.
5. Kurze, *Annales regni Francorum*, pp. 114, 131.
6. *Expositio totius mundi et gentium*, trans. J. Rougé (Paris, 1966), sec. 20.
7. For an account of this, see E. Lévi-Provençal, *Histoire de l'Espagne musulmane*, 2d ed., 3 vols. (Paris, 1950–53), 1:225ff. For a description of the Eastern Christians' image of Islam, see A. Ducellier, *Le Miroir de l'Islam: Musulmans et Chrétiens d'Orient au Moyen Âge (VII-XIe siècles)* (Paris, 1971).
8. See the *Song of Roland*, ll. 3220–30.

9. Quote from William of Tyre, *L'Estoire de Éracles empereur et la conqueste de la terre d'outremer*, bk. 11, chap. 20, p. 487 in *Recueil des historiens des croisades: Historiens occidentaux*, vol. 1, pt. 1 (Paris, 1844). See also R. Grousset, *Histoire des croisades*, 3 vols. (Paris, 1934–36), 1:275–76; and J. LaMonte, "Crusade and Jihād," in *The Arab Heritage*, ed. N. A. Faris (Princeton, 1944), pp. 168–69.

10. Cited in E. Dreesbach, *Der Orient in der altfranzösischen Kreuzzugslitteratur* (Breslau, 1901), p. 10.

11. J. de Joinville, *The Life of St. Louis*, trans. R. Hague (London, 1955), chap. 56, sec. 280, p. 94; see also Dreesbach, *Der Orient*, p. 34; William of Tyre, *L'Estorie*, bk. 21, chap. 23, pp. 1043–44 in *Recueil des historiens des croisades*, vol. 1, pt. 2 (Paris, 1849).

12. R. W. Southern, *Western Views of Islam in the Middle Ages* (Cambridge, Mass., 1962), pp. 28–29.

13. *Gesta Dei per Francos*, bk. 1, caput 3 in *Patrologia Latina*, ed. J. P. Migne (Paris, 1853), vol. 156, col. 689; Southern, *Western Views of Islam*, p. 31.

14. Der Stricker, *Karl der Grosse*, ed. K. Bartsch (Quedlinburg, 1857), p. 111, l. 4205; see also H. Adolf, "Christendom and Islam in the Middle Ages: New Light on 'Grail Stone' and 'Hidden Host,'" *Speculum* 32 (1957): 105.

15. Y. Pellat, and C. Pellat, "L'Idée de Dieu chez les 'Sarrasins' des chansons de geste," *Studia Islamica* 22 (1965): 5–42.

16. U. Monneret de Villard, *Lo Studio dell'Islam in Europa nel XII e nel XIII secolo*, no. 110 of *Studi e Testi* (Vatican, 1944), pp. 2–3.

17. Books, translations, and translators were not the only means of contact with the East. According to the Anglo-Norman monk and historian Orderic Vital (d. after 1143), the future king of France, Louis VI, was poisoned by his stepmother, Bertrade d'Anjou, around the year 1100.

Since all the French doctors were incapable of curing the prince, there arrived from Barbary [North Africa, in this context, rather, Muslim Spain] a hairy and bearded person [*quidam hirsutus*] who performed an operation on the young man whose state was deemed hopeless. Through the grace of God, the cure met with success despite the resentment of the native doctors [i.e., the French doctors]. This person had spent a long time among the pagans [Muslims] and had carefully learned from their teachers the most profound secrets of the art of medicine. In effect, prolonged philosophical research had elevated their knowledge of things above the level of all the barbarian scholars. And so, the prince recovered (*Orderic Vital ... Historiæ ecclesiasticæ libri tredecim ...* , 5 vols., ed. A. Le Prévost [Paris, 1838–55], vol. 4, bk. 11, sec. 9, pp. 196–97).

A French translation of the entire episode is found in A. Zeller, and P. Luchaire, *Les Premiers Capétiens* (Paris, 1883), pp. 140–44.

18. Quote from Petri Venerabilis, "Epistola de Translatione Sua" in *Patrologia Latina*, ed. J. P. Migne (Paris, 1890), vol. 189, cols. 651–52; see also, Southern, *Western Views of Islam*, pp. 38–39; J. Leclercq, *Pierre le Vénérable* (Abbaye St. Wandrille, 1946), pp. 242–43.

19. See especially, M. T. d'Alverny, "Deux traductions latines du Coran au Moyen Âge," *Archives d'histoire doctrinale et littéraire du Moyen Âge* 22–23 (1947–48): 69–131; J. Kritzeck, *Peter the Venerable and Islam* (Princeton, 1964); and idem, "Robert of Ketton's Translation of the Qur'ān," *Islamic Quarterly* 2 (1955): 309–12.

20. See L. Minio-Paluello, "Aristotele dal mondo arabo a quello latino," *L'Occidente e l'Islam nell'alto Medioevo* in *Settimane di Studio del Centro italiano sull'alto Medioevo*, no. 12, vol. 2 (Spoleto, 1965), pp. 603–37.

21. Among others see, M. T. d'Alverny, "L'Introduction d'Avicenne en Occident," *Millénaire d'Avicenne, Revue du Caire* 141 (June 1951): 130–39; idem, "Notes sur les traductions médiévales d'Avicenne," *Archives d'histoire doctrinale et littéraire du Moyen Âge* 19 (1952): 337–58; M. Steinschneider, *Die europäischen Übersetzungen aus dem Arabischen bis Mitte des 17. Jahrhunderts* (1904–5; reprint Graz, 1966), pp. 16–32.

22. Roger Bacon, *Opus tertium*, vol. 1, sec. 1 of *Fr. Rogeri Bacon opera quædam hactenus inedita*, ed. J. Brewer (London, 1859), p. 32 as cited by R. de Vaux, "Notes et textes sur l'avicennisme latin aux confins des XIIe–XIIIe siècles," no. 20 of *Bibliothèque Thomiste* (Paris, 1934), p. 58n.9.

23. Roger Bacon, *The 'Opus majus' of Roger Bacon*, 3 vols., ed. J. Bridges (Oxford, 1897–1900), 2:227 as cited by de Vaux, "Notes et textes sur l'avicennisme," p. 60n.3.

24. See J. Jolivet, "Abélard et le Philosophe (Occident et Islam au XIIe siècle)," *Revue de l'histoire des religions* 164 (1963): 181–89. Interestingly, when Abélard became utterly frustrated with the theologians of his own country, he dreamed of going to a Muslim country where he thought he could at least earn his

livelihood and enjoy a certain legal status despite living among the enemies of Christ (see Abélard, *Historia calamitatum*, ed. J. Monfrin [Paris, 1959], pp. 97–98; and *The Story of Abelard's Adversities*, ed. and trans. J. Muckle [Toronto, 1954], p. 56); R. Roques, *Structures théologiques, de la Gnose à Richard de Saint-Victor* (Paris, 1962), p. 261.

25. Thomas Aquinas, *Summa contra Gentiles*, bk. 1, chap. 2.
26. Monneret de Villard, *Lo Studio dell'Islam*, pp. 36, and 37n.5.
27. See N. Daniel, *Islam and the West: The Making of an Image* (Edinburgh, 1960), pp. 65–66.
28. See, for example, de Vaux, "Notes et textes sur l'avicennisme latin."
29. Dreesbach, *Der Orient*, pp. 36–37, 67–68.
30. Dreesbach, *Der Orient*, pp. 40–41.
31. See E. Cerulli, *'Il libro della Scala' e la questione delle fonte arabo-spagnole della Divina Commedia* (Vatican, 1949), pp. 417–18.
32. Edited by T. van Erpe (Erpenius) with the chronicle of the Arab-Christian, al-Makīn, both of which are contained in *Historia saracenica* (Leiden, 1625).
33. See A. Udovich, "At the Origins of the Western Commenda: Islam, Israel, Byzantium," *Speculum* 37 (1962): 198–207.
34. A. Schaube, *Handelsgeschichte der römischen Völker des Mittelmeergebiets bis zum Ende der Kreuzzüge* (Munich, 1906), pp. 30–31.
35. Schaube, *Handelsgeschichte der römischen Völker*, p. 36.
36. I am drawing on the excellent work of R. Lopez, "L'Importanza del mondo islamico nella vita economica europea," *L'Occidente e l'Islam nell'alto Medioevo*, vol. 1, pp. 433–60.
37. Schaube, *Handelsgeschichte der römischen Völker*, pp. 33, 296–97; see also J. Le Goff, *Marchands et banquiers du Moyen Âge* (Paris, 1956), p. 75.
38. Lopez, "L'Importanza del mondo islamico," p. 460.
39. "Si in fide Christi et Christianitate sancta semper firmi fuissent." R. Grousset has some misgivings about this passage. He wonders how this crusader could know that the ancestors of the Seljuks had leanings toward Nestorianism (*Histoire des croisades*, 1:36n.1). A more likely explanation is that there was a vague notion that all the lands of Islam had once belonged to Christianity and that all who inhabited those lands and who were not pure Arabs must be descendants of Christian apostates.

40. *Histoire anonyme de la première croisade*, ed. and trans. L. Bréhier (Paris, 1924), pp. 50–53.

41. See Grousset, *Histoire des croisades*, 3:28–29.

42. The *Novellino*, dating from the second half of the thirteenth century, offers as a model: "Saladin . . . , sultan, very noble lord, valiant and generous" (soldano, nobilissimo signore, prode e largo), who directs reproaches against the Christians during a truce; being heartbroken by their contempt for the poor and their impiety, he again takes up arms. Otherwise he would have become a Christian (sec. 25). This story predates this text.

43. S. Duparc-Quioc, *Le Cycle de la croisade* (Paris, 1955), pp. 128–30. See G. Paris, "La Légende de Saladin," *Journal des Savants* (1893), pp. 284–85, 364–65, 428–29, 486–87 (also published separately under the same title in Paris, 1893); Daniel, *Islam and the West*, pp. 199–200; L. S. Crist, ed., *Saladin, suite et fin du deuxième cycle de la croisade* (Geneva, 1972).

44. Paris, "La Légende de Saladin," p. 34. See also G. Paris, *La Littérature française au Moyen Âge*, 5th ed. (Paris, 1913), sec. 87, p. 135–36.

45. See D. C. Munro, "The Western Attitude toward Islam during the Period of the Crusades," *Speculum* 6 (1931): 339.

46. Munro, "The Western Attitude toward Islam," p. 339; Grousset, *Histoire des croisades*, 3:83.

47. Regarding this concept, see M. Rodinson, "Problématique de l'étude des rapports entre Islam et communisme" in *Colloque sur la sociologie musulmane, Actes 11–14 septembre 1961* (Brussels, n.d.), pp. 119–49. This paper is reprinted and slightly modified in: idem, *Marxism and the Muslim World*, trans. H. J. Matthews (New York, 1981); see also idem, "Marxist Sociology and Marxist Ideology," *Diogenes*, no. 64 (1968): 57–90, revised in *Marx and Contemporary Scientific Thought/Marx et la pensée scientifique contemporaine* (The Hague, 1969), pp. 67–92.

48. See E. Kantorowicz, *Frederick the Second, 1194–1250*, trans., E. Lorimer (London, 1931), pp. 128–32, 183–89, 195, 339–42.

49. Kantorowicz, *Frederick the Second*, p. 187; Grousset, *Histoire des croisades*, 3:271–72.

50. See Kantorowicz, *Frederick the Second*, pp. 499–500; L. Massignon, "La Légende 'de tribus impostoribus' et ses origines islamiques," *Revue de l'histoire des religions* 82 (1920): 74–78; reprinted in his *Opera Minora*, 3 vols., ed. Y. Moubarac (Beirut, 1963), 1:82–85; Southern, *Western Views of Islam*, p. 75n.16.

The parallel (but in a more positive sense) to the story of the three impostors is the story of the three rings, which appears in the *Novellino* (sec. 73). In this story, Saladin, in need of money, tries to entrap a wealthy Jew. He asks the man to tell him which is the true religion, expecting him to say Judaism. But the Jew saves himself by relating the tale of a man who owned a valuable ring that was coveted by his three sons. He could not decide which one should inherit it so he had a jeweler make two beautiful copies of the original. He then gave each son a ring, and each believed he had the original. The same story is found in the *Decameron* of Boccaccio (first day, tale 3); and in G. Lessing's dramatic poem *Nathan der Weise* (1779).

51. See Daniel, *Islam and the West*, pp. 195–96, and passim.
52. Wolfram von Eschenbach, *Parzival*, stanza 108.
53. Von Eschenbach, *Parzival*, stanza 782.
54. Von Eschenbach, *Parzival*, stanza 453.
55. See H. Goetz, "Der Orient der Kreuzzüge in Wolframs *Parzival*," *Archiv für Kulturgeschichte* 49 (1967): 1–42; M. Plessner, "Orientalistische Bemerkungen zu religionshistorischen Deutungen von Wolframs *Parzival*," *Medium Aevum* 36 (1967): 253–66.
56. Jean de Plano Carpini, *History of the Mongols*, chap. 8 in *The Mongol Mission: Narratives and Letters of of the Franciscan Missionaries in Mongolia and China in the Thirteenth and Fourteenth Centuries*, edited by C. Dawson (New York, 1955), p. 45.
57. See Southern, *Western Views of Islam*, pp. 42–43.
58. See *The Travels of William de Rubruquis* in J. Pinkerton, *A General Collection of the Best and Most Interesting Travels in All Parts of the World* (London, 1811), pp. 79–82.
59. Southern, *Western Views of Islam*, pp. 52–53.
60. Dante, *Inferno*, canto 4, ll. 129, 143–44.
61. See Southern, *Western Views of Islam*, pp. 77–78.
62. Southern, *Western Views of Islam*, pp. 75–76.
63. *Canterbury Tales, General Prologue*, ll. 429–34.
64. See H. Schipperges, *Ideologie und Historiographie des Arabismus* (Wiesbaden, 1961).
65. Petrarch, *Senilia*, 12, Ep. 2 in *Opera Latina* ... , ed. (Basle, 1581), p. 913. See E. Cerulli, "Petrarca e gli Arabi," *Rivista di cultura classica e medioevale* 7 (1965): 331–36.
66. Southern, *Western Views of Islam*, p. 67.
67. Regarding this, see Southern, *Western Views of Islam*, pp. 86–87.

68. See, for example, Philippe de Commynes, *Mémoires*, bk. 7, chap. 17 in *Historiens et chroniqueurs du Moyen Âge*, 2d ed., ed. A. Pauphilet, and E. Pognon (Paris, 1958), p. 1345; idem, *Mémoires*, 3 vols., ed. J. Calmette, and G. Durville (Paris, 1924–25), 3:103.

69. See J. R. Hale, "The Renaissance" in *The Cambridge Modern History*, vol. 1 (Cambridge, 1957), p. 264.

70. See Commynes, *Mémoires*, ed. Pauphilet, and Pognon, bk. 7, chap. 19, p. 1351; idem, *Mémoires*, ed. Calmette, and Durville, 3:116.

71. J. Burchard, *Johannis Burchari Argentinensis capelle pontificie sacrorum rituum magistri diarium ... (1483–1506)*, 3 vols., ed. L. Thuasne (Paris, 1883–85), 2:202–3; idem, *Liber notarum*, ed. E. Celani, 2 vols. (Città di Castello, 1907–14), 1:547; idem, *Le Journal de Jean Burchard, évêque et cérémoniaire au Vatican*, trans. J. Turmel (Paris, 1932), pp. 175–76.

72. See the note by J. Turmel in Burchard, *Le Journal de Jean Burchard*, p. 222.

73. Hale, "The Renaissance," p. 265.

74. J. Parry, "The Ottoman Empire, 1481–1520, in *The Cambridge Modern History*, vol. 1 (Cambridge, 1957), p. 403. The friendly relations between Milan and the Turks were by then longstanding, having been secured by a common opposition to Venice and reinforced when Milan dominated Venice's old rival, Genoa. A century earlier, their relations even influenced French domestic politics. In the words of a writer of the period, Sultan Bāyezīd I (Bajazet) and Duke Gian Galeazzo Visconti (1385–1407), great-grandfather of Ludovic, "shared a great mutual love although they never met one another" (see the anonymous, "Relation de la croisade de Nicopolis," in *Oeuvres de Froissart*, 25 vols., ed. J. Kervyn de Lettenhove [Brussels, 1867–77], 15:492). It was also known that Duke Gian Galeazzo kept up on news at the French court through his daughter, Valentina (1366–1408), who was married to Louis d'Orléans, brother of King Charles VI. When the "Crusaders" led by Jean, Count of Nevers (1371–1419) were defeated by Bāyezīd at Nicopolis in 1396, the sultan freed the Burgundian knight Jacques de Heilly so that he could take the news of the sultan's victory to Paris along with the sultan's ransom demands. Bāyezīd also ordered the knight to travel by way of Milan so he could greet Gian Galeazzo. The Duke of Burgundy (father of count Jean) on two occasions sent letters to the

Duke of Milan asking that he commend his son to the sultan's
benevolence (see J. Delaville Le Roulx, *La France en Orient au
XIVe siècle*, 2 vols. [Paris, 1886], 1:291, 301, 304.

This did not prevent Count Jean, who would become
Duke Jean sans Peur, from blaming the Crusaders' defeat on
Valentina's information and its transmission via Milan to the
Turks. He returned full of bitterness after spending two long
years in a Turkish prison where he saw his companions suffer
and die. This, and other motives, fueled his fierce hatred of
Louis d'Orléans and eventually led him to order his murder on
the evening of 23 November 1407 on the Rue Vieille-du-Temple
in Paris (see Froissart, *Oeuvres de Froissart*, 15:354; J. d'Avout,
La Querelle des Armagnacs et des Bourguignons [Paris, 1943],
pp. 43ff). Two decades later, relations were still very cordial between Gian Galeazzo's son, Duke Filippo Maria (1412–47), and
Bāyezīd's grandson, Murād II (1421–51). They called each other
brothers and exchanged gifts. In 1433, an ambassador from Milan
tried, as part of the anti-Venetian campaign, to pressure Murād
to stop fighting Sigismund (1368–1437), the German emperor
and king of Hungary, and to make broad concessions on disputed territories to him. The sultan publicly replied that "out of
love for him [i.e., Duke Filippo Maria], he had refrained from major conquests of the lands of the kingdom of Hungary" and that
was quite enough. Nevertheless, soon after this, Murād ceased
fighting in Transylvania and sent a peace ambassador to Sigismund bearing rich gifts to honor his coronation in Rome in 1433
(see B. de La Brocquière, *Le Voyage d'Outremer*, ed. C. Schéfer
(Paris, 1892), pp. 191–96; G. Romano, "Filippo Maria Visconti e
i Turchi," *Archivio Storico Lombardo* 17 [1890]: 585–618. For an
overview, see D. M. Vaughan, *Europe and the Turk: A Pattern of
Alliances, 1350–1700* (Liverpool, 1954).

75. See N. Daniel, *Islam, Europe and Empire* (Edinburgh, 1966), p.
    12.
76. J. Burckhardt, *Die Kultur der Renaissance in Italien* (Basel,
    1860) (English trans. of first part: *The Civilization of the Renais-
    sance in Italy*, trans. S. Middlemore [London, 1944], pp. 59–60);
    see also, F. Babinger, *Mahomet II le Conquérant et son temps*
    (Paris, 1954), pp. 396–97.
77. Daniel, *Islam, Europe and Empire*, pp. 4–10.
78. V. Segesvary's dissertation, *L'Islam et la Réforme: Étude sur
    l'attitude des Réformateurs zurichois envers l'Islam (1510–1550)*

(Lausanne, 1977), contains a wealth of information and is not limited to the Reformation in Zurich nor even to Switzerland.

79. See R. Schwoebel, *The Shadow of the Crescent: The Renaissance Image of the Turk (1453–1517)* (Nieuwkoop, 1967), pp. 148, 189.

80. See Voltaire, *Le Siècle de Louis XIV*, chap. 14; F. Grenard, *Grandeur et décadence de l'Asie* (Paris, 1939), p. 130.

81. Schwoebel, *The Shadow of the Crescent*, p. 188, cf. p. 180.

82. See, for example, Machiavelli, *Il Principe*, chap. 19 where he compares the Ottoman regime with the rule of the Mamluks, and in turn, the Mamluks with the papacy as an example of elective monarchy; see also *Il Principe*, chap. 4; and idem, *Discorsi sulla prima Deca di Tito Livio*, bk. 2, foreword.

83. Schwoebel, *The Shadow of the Crescent*, p. 178.

84. See, for example, G. Levi della Vida, "Fonti orientali dell'Isabella ariostesca" in *Anedotti e svaghi arabi e non arabi* (Milan, 1959), pp. 170–90.

85. Shakespeare, *Othello*, act 3, sc. 4, ll. 53–59.

86. *Segraisiana*, cited by G. Lanson, *Théâtre choisi de Racine*, 7th ed. (Paris, 1910), p. 437.

87. See J. Fück, *Die arabischen Studien in Europa bis in den Anfang des 20. Jahrhunderts* (Leipzig, 1955), pp. 36–37. More information regarding G. Postel can be found in F. Secret, *Les Kabbalistes chrétiens de la Renaissance* (Paris, 1964), pp. 171–72, and passim; Y. Moubarac, *Recherches sur la pensée chrétienne et l'Islam* (Beirut, 1977), p. 45.

88. See G. Preti, *Storia del pensiero scientifico* (Milan, 1957), pp. 278, 287.

89. Compare this to the references to classical Marxist works (Marx, etc.) that are dutifully scattered throughout the most specialized scientific works published in the U.S.S.R.

90. A fact admitted by Fück, *Die arabischen Studien in Europa*, p. 98.

91. See particularly, M. Abdel-Halim, *Antoine Galland, sa vie et son oeuvre* (Paris, 1964).

92. See especially, M. Dufrenoy, *L'Orient romanesque en France, 1704–1789*, vols. 1–2 (Montreal, 1946–47), and vol. 3 (Amsterdam, 1975).

93. R. Simon, *Histoire critique … par le sieur de Moni* (Frankfurt, 1684), chap. 15; cf. his *Lettres choisies*, 4 vols. (Amsterdam, 1730), 3:245–46, 258–59; J. Steinmann, *Richard Simon et les origines de l'exégèse biblique* (Paris, 1960), pp. 157–58; cf., M. Rodin-

son, "Richard Simon et la dédogmatisation," *Les Temps Modernes*, no. 202 (March 1963), pp. 1700–1701.

94. A. Reland, *De religione mohammedica* ... (Utrecht, 1705).

95. See T. W. Arnold, "Toleration (Muhammadan)" in *Encyclopaedia of Religion and Ethics*, ed. J. Hastings, (Edinburgh, 1921), vol. 12, pp. 365–69; F. Babinger, *Mahomet II*, pp. 143–44.

96. See Voltaire, Robertson, and Herder. Cf., H. Schipperges, *Ideologie und Historiographie*, pp. 29, 34. This theme is developed to the greatest extent at the end of the century by the Spanish Jesuit, Juan Andrés (1740–1817) in his book, *Dell'origine, progressi, e stato attuale d'ogni letteratura* ... , 7 vols. (Parma, 1782–99), see the Spanish translation by Carlos Andrés (Madrid, 1784–1806).

97. Daniel, *Islam and the West*, p. 288.

98. A vacillation rarely understood by either Muslims or Orientalists! Compare his tragedy, *Mahomet* and, for example, chaps. 6, 27, and 44 of *Essai sur les Moeurs*. Late in life, Voltaire made the point himself in the article "Mahométans" in his *Dictionnaire philosophique*. The work of D. Hadidi, *Voltaire et l'Islam* (Paris, 1974) offers a simplistic and apologetic analysis but has the advantage of assembling a number of scattered texts.

99. Fück, *Die arabischen Studien in Europa*, pp. 108–24.

100. See P. Hazard, *La Crise de la conscience européenne (1680–1715)*, 2 vols. (Paris, 1935), 1:22.

101. M. Petrocchi, "Il mito di Maometto in Boulainviliers," *Rivista storica italiana* 60 (1948): 367–77.

102. Daniel, *Islam, Europe and Empire*, pp. 14–15.

103. Montesquieu, *L'Esprit des lois*, bk. 3, chap. 9.

104. T. Hope, *Anastasius, or, Memoirs of a Modern Greek*, 2d ed., 3 vols. (London, 1820), 2:376.

105. See B. Lewis, "Some English Travellers in the East," *Middle Eastern Studies* 4.3 (April 1968): 296–315; Daniel, *Islam, Europe and Empire*, pp. 13–14, 20–21.

106. J. J. Rousseau, *Confessions*, bk. 4.

107. Hazard, *La Crise de la conscience européenne*, 1:20, 23–24; Dufrenoy, *L'Orient romanesque en France*, pp. 157–58.

108. See the work by J. Gaulmier, *L'Idéologue Volney* (Beirut, 1951), which the author condensed in his *Un grand témoin de la Révolution et de l'Empire, Volney* (Paris, 1959).

109. See Fück, *Die arabischen Studien in Europa*, pp. 135–40; and R. Schwab, *La Renaissance orientale* (Paris, 1950), pp. 208–9.

110. *West-östlicher Divan*, Noten und Abhandlungen, Einleitung.
111. *West-östlicher Divan*, trans. H. Lichtenberger (Paris, 1940). See also Schwab, *La Renaissance orientale*, p. 386.
112. F. Schlegel, *Athenaeum* (Berlin, 1798–1800) cited by R. Schwab, *La Renaissance orientale*, p. 20.
113. See G. Lukacs, *Brève histoire de la littérature allemande (du XVI-IIe siècle à nos jours)*, trans. L. Goldman, and M. Butor (Paris, 1949), pp. 83–84.
114. This term is often employed by writers of the period, see Schwab, *La Renaissance orientale*.
115. Fück, *Die arabischen Studien in Europa*, p. 141.
116. Fück, *Die arabischen Studien in Europa*, pp. 140–58; H. Dehérain, *Silvestre de Sacy, ses contemporains et ses disciples* (Paris, 1938).
117. *Dragoman*: "an interpreter chiefly of Arabic, Turkish or Persian employed especially in the Near East" (*Webster's Ninth Collegiate*). It is an old loan word from Arabic *turjumân*.
118. This journal also had a rhymed Arabic title as well as a French title—*Mines de l'Orient exploitées par une société d'amateurs*. Its very pointed epigraph was a verse from the Qur'ān: "Say: God is the master of the East and the West. He guides whom he wishes on the right path" (2:136/42).
119. Cf., V. V. Barthold, *La Découverte de l'Asie*, trans. B. Nikitine (Paris, 1947), pp. 264–65; Fück, *Die arabischen Studien in Europa*, pp. 155, 195–96; B. M. Dantsig, "Iz istorii izutshenija Blizhnego Vostoka v Rossii," *Otsherki po istorii russkogo vostokovedenija* (Moscow, 1959), vol. 4, pp. 3–38; I. J. Kratshkovskij, *Otsherki po istorii russkoj arabistiki* (Moscow, 1950), pp. 73–74 (German trans. by O. Mehlitz, *Die russische Arabistik, Umrisse ihrer Entwicklung* (Leipzig, 1957), pp. 69–70.
120. *Giaour*, a popular word of the period (Byron published his poem, *The Giaour*, in 1813), is a transcription of a Turkish term "of contempt formerly applied to Christians in the same way Christians used 'infidel' in Europe to designate Muslims" (D. Kélékian, *Dictionnaire turc-français* [Constantinople, 1911], p. 1007.
121. Detailed information and references regarding this attitude can be found mostly in the work by Daniel, *Islam, Europe and Empire*. Daniel's explanation of these attitudes should be improved by the observations of A. Hourani in his review of Daniel's *Islam, Europe and Empire* in *Middle Eastern Studies* 4.3 (April 1968): 325–26.

122. Especially significant is the book by Abbot Rouquette of the Société des missions africaines of Lyons, *Les sociétés secrètes chez les musulmans* (Paris, 1899).

123. Ernest Renan leans in this direction, although with some oscillations. See, above all, Renan's famous lecture of 29 March 1883 at the Sorbonne, *L'Islamisme et la science* (Paris, 1883). This attitude was pushed to its limit by a militant Greek anti-Semite writing under the name D. Kimon, who published the eloquently titled book, *La Pathologie de l'Islam et les moyens de le détruire* (Paris, 1897); he also wrote the anti-Jewish work, *La Politique israélite, étude psychologique* (Paris, 1889).

124. Examples can be found in Daniel, *Islam, Europe and Empire*, pp. 385–86, and passim.

125. J. J. Waardenburg, *L'Islam dans le miroir de l'Occident* (Paris, 1963), pp. 102–6.

126. *Geschichte der herrschenden Ideen des Islams* (1868; reprinted, Hildesheim, 1961), p. xvii.

127. T. Stoddard, *The New World of Islam* (New York, 1921), pp. 129–30.

128. Stoddard, *The New World of Islam*, p. 354.

129. Especially typical is Sidi-Bel-Abbès's famous letter written to the secretariat of the French Communist Party by the Communist militants of Algeria, which was published for the first time in H. Carrère d'Encausse, and S. Schram's *Le Marxisme et l'Asie 1853–1964* (Paris, 1965), pp. 268–71.

130. "Good work, but beware of the picturesque and of Romanticism! " This advice was given by the Russian Communist journalist Maroussia, to the French Communist Paul Vaillant-Couturier at the train station in Tashkent when Vaillant-Couturier was about to tour Uzbekistan (P. Vaillant-Couturier, *Les bâtisseurs de la vie nouvelle*, vol. 2: *Au pays de Tamerlan* (Paris, 1932), pp. 9–10. On pages 11–12 of this work, the author declares that the words of Maroussia should be etched in his mind during the entire journey.

131. See A. A. Bennigsen, and C. Quelquejay, *Les Mouvements nationaux chez les musulmans de Russie*, vol. 1: *Le "Sultangaliévisme" au Tatarstan* (Paris, 1960); A. A. Bennigsen, S. E. Wimbush, *Muslim National Communism in the Soviet Union: A Revolutionary Strategy for the Colonial World* (Chicago, 1979).

132. See M. Rodinson, *Marxism and the Muslim World*, trans. M. Pallis (London 1979), pp. 133ff.

133. Typical of this attitude is the work by the theologian C. J. Ledit, *Mahomet, Israël et le Christ* (Paris, 1956).

134. See my introduction to the work of R. Dagorn, *La Geste d'Ismaël d'après l'onomastique et la tradition arabes* (Geneva, 1980).

135. The first conference of Islamists devoted to sociology was held in Brussels in 1961 and produced *Colloque sur la sociologie musulmane, Actes, 11–14 septembre 1961* (Brussels, n.d.).

136. See the article by C. Cahen in which he proposes a research program for the field of social and economic history, "L'Histoire économique et sociale de l'Orient musulman médieval" *Studia Islamica* 3 (1955): 93–115. The first conference devoted specifically to the economic history of the Muslim world in the medieval, modern, and contemporary periods was held in London in 1967 and produced *Studies in the Economic History of the Middle East from the Rise of Islam to the Present Day*, ed. M. Cook (London, 1970). Several pioneers in this respect, although their approaches vary widely, are Jean Sauvaget, Bernard Lewis, and Claude Cahen.

137. Particularly enlightening is the article of B. Farès, "Des difficultés d'ordre linguistique, culturel et social que rencontre un écrivain arabe moderne, spécialement en Égypte," *Revue des études islamiques* 10 (1936): 221–42. The problems affecting writers also apply to researchers in the field of social sciences.

138. A. Abdel-Malek does not take this sufficiently into account in his critique of European Orientalism, which, nonetheless, presents certain valid arguments (see his "Orientalism in Crisis," *Diogenes*, no. 44 [1963]: 103–40; cf., C. Cahen's letter in response in *Diogenes*, no. 49 [1965]: 135–38; and F. Gabrieli, "Apology for Orientalism," *Diogenes*, no. 50 [1965]: 128–36.)

139. See the figures for this in J. Chesneaux, "La Recherche marxiste et le réveil contemporain de l'Asie et de l'Afrique," *La Pensée* 95 (1961): 15–28.

140. See the early work of a very enlightened amateur, F. Grenard, *Grandeur et decadence de l'Asie*. In the same sense, see B. Lewis, "The Mongols, the Turks and the Muslim Polity," *Transactions of the Royal Historical Society*, 5th series, vol. 18 (1968): 49–68.

Toward a New Approach to Arab and Islamic Studies

1. J. Mohl, *27 ans d'histoire des études orientales*, 2 vols. (Paris, 1879–80), 1:44.

2. Mohl, *27 ans d'histoire*, 1:5–6.
3. Mohl, *27 ans d'histoire*, 1:25–26.
4. R. Levy, *An Introduction to the Sociology of Islam* (London, 1931–33); idem, *The Social Structure of Islam* (Cambridge, 1957).
5. C. A. O. van Nieuwenhuijze, *Sociology of the Middle East: A Stocktaking and Interpretation* (Leiden, 1971).
6. *The Trend in Middle East Studies as Illustrated by the Dutch Case*, lecture delivered to the Dutch Association for the Study of the Middle East and Islam (Leiden, 1976).
7. Hippocrates *Aphorisms* 1.1.

Select Bibliography

The works listed are not intended to provide a complete or even partial bibliography of the issues discussed in this book. They are simply the works used to support the arguments presented.

Abdel-Halim, M. *Antoine Galland, sa vie et son oeuvre.* Paris, 1964.

Abdel-Malek, A. "Orientalism in Crisis." *Diogenes,* no. 44 (1963): 103–40.

Abélard, P. *The Story of Abelard's Adversities.* Edited by J. Muckle. Toronto, 1954.

———. *Historia calamitatum.* Edited by J. Monfrin. Paris, 1959

Adolf, H. "Christendom and Islam in the Middle Ages: New Light on 'Grail Stone' and 'Hidden Host.'" *Speculum* 32 (1957): 103–15.

d'Alverny, M. T. "Deux traductions latines du Coran au Moyen Âge." *Archives d'histoire doctrinale et littéraire du Moyen Âge* 22–23 (1947–48): 69–131.

———. "L'Introduction d'Avicenne en Occident." *Millénaire d'Avicenne, Revue du Caire* 141 (June 1951):130–39.

———. "Notes sur les traductions médiévales d'Avicenne." *Archives d'histoire doctrinale et littéraire du Moyen Âge* 19 (1952): 337–58.

Andrés, Juan. *Dell'origine, progressi, e stato attuale d'ogni letteratura....* 7 vols. Parma, 1782–99. Spanish translation by Carlos Andrés, *Origen, progresos y estado actual de toda la literatura,* Madrid, 1784–1806.

Annales regni Francorum. In *Scriptores rerum Germanicarum in usum scholarum.* Edited by F. Kurze. Hanover, 1895.

Arnold, T. W. "Toleration (Muhammadan)." In *Encyclopedia of Religion and Ethics*. Edited by J. Hastings. Vol. 12, pp. 365–69. Edinburgh, 1921.

d'Avout, J. *La Querelle des Armagnacs et des Bourguignons*. Paris, 1943.

Babinger, F. *Mehmed der Eroberer und siene Zeit*. Munich, 1953. Translated into French by H. E. del Medico. *Mahomet II le Conquérant et son temps*. Paris, 1954.

Bacon, Roger. *Opus tertium*. Vol. 1, sec. 1 of *Fr. Rogeri Bacon opera quædam hactenus inedita*. Edited by J. Brewer. London, 1859.

——— . *The 'Opus majus' of Roger Bacon*. 3 vols. Edited by J. Bridges. Oxford, 1899–1900.

Barthold, V. V. *La Découverte de l'Asie*. Translated by B. Nikitine. Paris, 1947.

Bede, the Venerable. See Colgrave, B., and R. Mynors.

Bennigsen, A. A., and C. Quelquejay. *Le "Sultangaliévisme" au Tatarstan*. Vol. 1 of *Les Mouvements nationaux chez les musulmans de Russie*. Paris, 1960–64.

Benningsen, A. A., and S. E. Wimbush. *Muslim National Communism in the Soviet Union: A Revolutionary Strategy for the Colonial World*. Chicago, 1979.

Broquière, Bertandon, de la. *Le Voyage d'Outremer*. Edited by C. Schefer. Paris, 1892.

Burchard, J. *Johannis Burchardi Argentinensis capelle pontificie sacrorum rituum magistri diarium ... (1483–1506)*. 3 vols. Edited by L. Thuasne. Paris, 1883–85.

——— . *Liber notarum*. 2 vols. Edited by E. Celani. Città di Castello, 1907–14.

——— . *The Diary of John Burchard of Strasburg. . . .* Translated by A. Mathew. London, 1910.

——— . *Le Journal de Jean Burchard, évêque et cérémoniaire au Vatican*. Translated by J. Turmel. Paris, 1932.

Burckhardt, J. *Die Kultur der Renaissance in Italien*. Basel, 1860. English translation by S. Middlemore, *The Civilization of the Renaissance in Italy*, London, 1944.

Cahen, C. "L'Histoire économique et sociale de l'Orient musulman médiéval." *Studia Islamica* 3 (1955): 93–115.

——— . "Response to A. Abdel-Malek." *Diogenes*, no. 49 (1965): 135–38.

Carrère d'Encausse, H., and S. Schram. *Le Marxisme et l'Asie 1853–1964*. Paris, 1965.

Cerulli, E. *Il "Libro della Scala" e la questione delle fonte arabo-spagnole della Divina Commedia*. Vatican, 1949.

———. "Petrarca e gli Arabi." *Rivista di cultura classica e medioevale* 7 (1965): 331–36.

Chesneaux, J. "La Recherche marxiste et le réveil contemporain de l'Asie et de l'Afrique." *La Pensée* 95 (1961): 15–28.

Colgrave, B., and R. Mynors, eds., and trans. *Bede's Ecclesiastical History of the English People*. Oxford, 1969.

Commynes, Philippe, de. *Mémoires*. 3 vols. Edited by J. Calmette, and G. Durville. Paris, 1924–25.

———. *Mémoires*. In *Historiens et chroniqueurs du Moyen Âge*. 2d ed. Edited by A. Pauphilet, and E. Pognon. Paris, 1958.

Cook, M., ed. *Studies in the Economic History of the Middle East from the Rise of Islam to the Present Day*. Oxford, 1970.

Dagron, R. *La Geste d'Ismaël d'après l'onomastique et la tradition arabes*. Geneva, 1980.

Daniel, N. *Islam and the West: The Making of an Image*. Edinburgh, 1960.

———. *Islam, Europe and Empire*. Edinburgh, 1966.

Dantsig, B. M. "Iz istorii izutshenija Blizhnego Vostoka v Rossii." *Otsherki po istorii russkogo vostokovedenija* 4 (1959): 3–38.

Dehérain, H. *Silvestre de Sacy, ses contemporains et ses disciples*. Paris, 1938.

Delaville Le Roulx, J. *La France en Orient au XIVe siècle*. 2 vols. Paris, 1886.

Djait, H. *L'Europe et l'Islam*. Paris, 1978.

Dreesbach, E. *Der Orient in der altfranzösischen Kreuzzugslitteratur*. Breslau, 1901.

Ducellier, A. *Le Miroir de l'Islam, Musulmans et Chrétiens d'Orient au Moyen Âge (VII–XIe siècles)*. Paris, 1971.

Dufrenoy, M. *L'Orient romanesque en France, 1704–1789*. Vols. 1 and 2. Montreal, 1946–47. Vol. 3. Amsterdam, 1975.

Duparc-Quioc, S. *Le Cycle de la Croisade*. Paris, 1955.

van Erpe (Erpenius), T., ed. *Historia saracenica*. Leiden, 1625.

Expositio totius mundi et gentium. Translated and edited by J. Rougé. Paris, 1966.

Farès, B. "Des Difficultés d'ordre linguistique, culturel et social que rencontre un écrivain arabe moderne, spécialement en Égypte." *Revue des études islamiques* 10 (1936): 221–42.

Fredegar. See Wallace-Hadrill, J. M.

Froissart, J. *Oeuvres de Froissart.* 25 vols. Edited by K. de Lettenhove. Brussels, 1867–77.

Fück, J. *Die arabischen Studien in Europa bis in den Anfang des 20
Jahrhunderts.* Leipzig, 1955.

Gabrieli, F. "Apology for Orientalism." *Diogenes*, no. 50 (1965): 128–
36.

Gaulmier, J. *L'Idéologue Volney.* Beirut, 1951.

——— . *Un Grand témoin de la Révolution et de l'Empire, Volney.*
Paris, 1959.

Gesta Dei per Francos. In *Patrologia Latina.* Vol. 156. Edited by J. P.
Migne. Paris, 1844.

Gesta Francorum: Histoire anonyme de la première Croisade. Edited
and translated by L. Bréhier. Paris, 1924.

Goetz, H. "Der Orient der Kreuzzüge in Wolframs *Parzival.*" *Archiv
für Kulturgeschichte* 49 (1967): 1–42.

Grenard, F. *Grandeur et décadence de l'Asie.* Paris, 1939.

Grousset, R. *Histoire des Croisades.* 3 vols. Paris, 1934–36.

Hadidi, D. *Voltaire et l'Islam.* Paris, 1974.

Hale, J. *The Renaissance.* Vol. 1 of *The Cambridge Modern History.*
Edited by G. Potter. Cambridge, 1957–79.

Hazard, P. *La Crise de la conscience européenne (1680–1715).* 2 vols.
Paris, 1935.

Hope, T. *Anastasius, or, Memoirs of a Modern Greek.* 2d ed. 3 vols.
London, 1820.

Hourani, A. Review of *Islam, Europe and Empire* by N. Daniel. *Middle
Eastern Studies* 4.3 (1968): 325–26.

Joinville, J. de. *The History of St. Louis* Translated by R. Hague.
London, 1955.

Jolivet, J. "Abélard et le philosophe (Occident et Islam au XIIe
siècle." *Revue de l'histoire des religions* 164 (1963): 181–89.

Kantorowicz, E. *Kaiser Friedrich der Zweite.* 1927–31. Reprint. Dus-
seldorf, 1963. English translation by E. Lorimer, *Frederick the
Second, 1194–1250,* London, 1931.

Kimon, D. *La Pathologie de l'Islam et les moyens de le détruire.* Paris,
1897.

——— . *La Politique israélite, étude psychologique.* Paris, 1889.

Kratshkovskij, I. J. *Otsherki po istorii russkoj arabistiki.* Moscow,
1950. German translation by O. Mehlitz. *Die russische Arabistik,
Umrisse ihrer Entwicklung,* Leipzig, 1959.

Kremer, A., von. *Geschichte der herrshenden Ideen des Islams.* 1868.
Reprint. Hildesheim, 1961.

Kritzeck, J. "Robert of Ketton's Translation of the Qur'ān." *Islamic Quarterly* 2 (1955): 309–12.

———. *Peter the Venerable and Islam.* Princeton, 1964.

La Brocquière, Betrandon de. *Le Voyage d'Outremer.* Edited by C. Shafer, Paris, 1892.

LaMonte, J. "Crusade and Jihād." In *The Arab Heritage*, pp. 159–98. Edited by N. A. Faris. Princeton, 1944.

Lanson, G. *Théâtre choisi de Racine.* 7th ed. Paris, 1910.

Leclercq, J. *Pierre le Vénérable.* Abbaye St. Wandrille, 1946.

Ledit, C. J. *Mahomet, Israël et le Christ.* Paris, 1956.

Le Goff, J. *Marchands et banquiers du Moyen Âge.* Paris, 1956.

Lévi-Provençal, E. *Histoire de l'Espagne musulmane.* 2d ed. 2 vols. Paris, 1950.

Lévy, R. *An Introduction to the Sociology of Islam.* London, 1931–33.

———. *The Social Structure of Islam.* Cambridge, 1957.

Lewis, B. "The Mongols, the Turks and the Muslim Polity." *Transactions of the Royal Historical Society* 5th series, vol. 18 (1968): 49–68.

———. "Some English Travellers in the East." *Middle Eastern Studies* 4.3 (April 1968): 296–315.

Lukacs, G. *Brève histoire de la littérature allemande (du XVIIIe siècle à nos jours).* Translated by L. Goldman, and M. Butor. Paris, 1949.

Marx and the Contemporary Scientific Thought/Marx et la pensée scientifique contemporaine. The Hague, 1969.

Massignon, L. "La Légende de *tribus impostoribus* et ses origines islamiques." *Revue de l'histoire des religions* 82 (1920): 74–78. Reprinted in his *Opera Minora*, 3 vols. Edited by Y. Moubarac. Beirut, 1963. Vol. 1, pp. 82–85.

Mohl, J. *27 ans d'histoire des études orientales.* 2 vols. Paris, 1879–80.

Monneret de Villard, U. *Lo Studio dell'Islam in Europa nel XII e nel XIII secolo.* No. 110 of *Studi e Testi.* Vatican, 1944.

Moubarac, Y. *Recherches sur la pensée chrétienne et l'Islam.* Beirut, 1977.

Munro, D. C. "The Western Attitude toward Islam during the Period of the Crusades." *Speculum* 6 (1931): 329–43.

van Nieuwenhuijze, C. A. O. *Sociology of the Middle East: A Stocktaking and Interpretation.* Leiden, 1971.

Novellino. Edited by E. Sicardi. Strasbourg, n.d.

Orderic Vital. *Historiæ ecclesiasticæ libri tredecim.* 5 vols. Edited by Le Prévost. Paris, 1838–55.

Paris, G. "La Légende de Saladin." *Journal des Savants* (May–August 1893). Also published separately as *La Légende de Saladin.* Paris, 1893.

————. *La Littérature française au Moyen Âge.* 5th ed. Paris, 1913.

Parry, J. "The Ottoman Empire, 1481–1520." In *The Cambridge Modern History.* Vol. 1, pp. 395–419. Cambridge, 1957.

Pellat, Y., and C. Pellat. "L'Idée de Dieu chez les 'Sarrasins' des Chansons de Geste." *Studia Islamica* 22 (1965): 5–42.

Petrarca, F. *Opera Latina....* Basle, 1581.

Petrocchi, M. "Il mitto di Maometto in Boulainviliers." *Rivista storica italiana* 60 (1948): 367–77.

Plano Carpini, John de. *History of the Mongols.* In *The Mongol Mission: Narratives and Letters of Franciscan Missionaries in Mongolia and China in the Thirteenth and Fourteenth Centuries.* Edited by C. Dawson. New York, 1955.

Plessner, M. "Orientalistische Bemerkungen zu religionshistorischen Deutungen von Wolframs *Parzival.*" *Medium Aevum* 36 (1967): 253–66.

Preti, G. *Storia del pensiero scientifico.* Milan, 1957.

Reland, A. *De religione mohammedica....* Utrecht, 1705.

Renan, E. *L'Islamisme et la science.* Paris, 1883.

Rodinson, M. "Racisme et ethnisme." *Pluriel* 3 (1957): 7–27.

————. "Problématique de l'étude des rapports entre Islam et communisme." *Colloque sur la sociologie musulmane, Actes, 11–14 septembre 1961.* Brussels, n.d.

————. "Richard Simon et la dédogmatisation." *Les Temps Modernes,* no. 202 (March 1963): 1700–1709.

————. "Marxist Sociology and Marxist Ideology." *Diogenes,* no. 64 (1968): 57–70. Revised in *Marx and Contemporary Thought/Marx et la pensée scientifique contemporaine.* The Hague, 1969.

————. "Nation et idéologie." In *Encyclopaedia universalis.* Vol. 11, pp. 571–75. Paris, 1968–74.

————. "Les Influences de la civilisation musulmane sur la civilisation européenne dans le domaine de la consommation et de la distraction." In *Convegno Internazionale, 9–15 Aprile 1969, Tema: Oriente e Occidente,* pp. 479–99. Rome, 1971.

————. *Marxisme et monde musulman.* Paris, 1972. Partial English translations by M. Pallis, *Marxism and the Muslim World,* London, 1979; and H. J. Matthews, *Marxism and the Muslim World,* New York, 1981.

————. "Dynamique de l'évolution interne et des influences externes dans l'histoire culturelle de la Méditerranée." In *Actes du premier Congrès d'études des cultures méditerranéennes d'influence arabo-berbère*, pp. 21–30. Algiers, 1973.

————. "The Western Image and Western Studies of Islam." In *The Legacy of Islam*. 2d ed., pp. 9–62. Edited by J. Schacht, and C. Bosworth. Oxford, 1974.

————. "Situation, acquis et problèmes de l'orientalisme islamisant." In *Le Mal de voir, ethnologie et orientalisme*, pp. 242–57. Paris, 1976.

————. *La Fascination de l'Islam, étapes du regard occidental sur le monde musulman*. Nijmegen, 1978.

Romano, G. "Filippo Maria Visconti e i Turchi." *Archivio Storico-Lombardo* 17 (1890): 585–618.

Roques, R. *Structures théologiques, de la Gnose à Richard de Saint-Victor*. Paris, 1962.

Rouquette, A. *Les Sociétés secrètes chez les musulmans*. Paris, 1899.

Said, Edward. *Orientalism*. New York, 1978.

Saladin, suite et fin du deuxième cycle de la Croisade. Edited by L. S. Crist. Geneva, 1972.

Schaube, A. *Handelsgeschichte der römischen Völker des Mittelmeergebiets bis zum Ende der Kreuzzüge*. Munich, 1906.

Schipperges, H. *Ideologie und Historiographie des Arabismus*. Wiesbaden, 1961.

Schwab, R. *La Renaissance orientale*. Paris, 1950.

Schwoebel, R. *The Shadow of the Crescent: The Renaissance Image of the Turk (1453–1517)*. Nieuwkoop, 1967.

Secret, F. *Les Kabbalistes chrétiens de la Renaissance*. Paris, 1964.

Segesvary, V. *L'Islam et la Réforme: Étude sur l'attitude des Réformateurs zurichois envers l'Islam (1510–1550)*. Lausanne, 1977.

Simon, R. *Histoire critique … par le Sieur de Moni*. Frankfurt, 1684.

————. *Lettres choisies*. 4 vols. Amsterdam, 1730.

Southern, R. W. *Western Views of Islam in the Middle Ages*. Cambridge, Mass., 1962.

Steinmann, J. *Richard Simon et les origines de l'exégèse biblique*. Paris, 1960.

Steinschneider, M. *Die europäischen Übersetzungen aus dem Arabischen bis Mitte des 17. Jahrunderts*. 1904–5. Reprint. Graz, 1966.

Stoddard, T. *The Rising Tide of Color against White World-Supremacy*. New York, 1920.

————. *The New World of Islam*. New York, 1921.

der Stricker. *Karl der Grosse.* Edited by K. Bartsch. Quedlinburg, 1857.

Udovich, A. "At the Origins of the Western Commenda: Islam, Israel, Byzantium." *Speculum* 37 (1962): 198–207.

Vaillant-Couturier, P. *Au pays de Tamerlan.* Vol. 2 of *Les Bâtisseurs de la vie nouvelle.* Paris, 1932.

Vaughan, D. M. *Europe and the Turk, a Pattern of Alliances, 1350–1700.* Liverpool, 1954.

Vaux, R., de. *Notes et textes sur l'avicennisme latin aux confins des XIIe–XIIIe siècles.* No. 20 of *Bibliothèque Thomiste.* Paris, 1934.

Waardenburg, J. J. *L'Islam dans le miroir de l'Occident.* Paris, 1963.

Wallace-Hadrill, J., ed. and trans. *Fredegarii chronicon: The Fourth Book of the Chronicle of Fredegar, with Its Continuations.* London, 1960.

Watt, W. "L'Influence de l'Islam sur l'Europe médiévale." *Revue des études islamiques* 40 (1972): 7–41, 297–327; and 41 (1973): 127–56.

William of Tyre. *L'Estoire de Éracles empereur et la conqueste de la terre d'outremer.* In *Recueil des historiens des croisades; historiens occidentaux.* Vol. 1, pts. 1 and 2. Paris, 1844.

———. *Guillaume de Tyr et ses continuateurs, texte français du XIIIe siècle.* Edited by P. Paris. Paris, 1879–80.

Index

Abélard, Peter, 17, 133–34n.24
Alvaro of Cordova, 6
Amari, Michele, 70
America. *See* United States
American Oriental Society, 56
Anawati, M. M., 105
Année sociologique, 108
Anthropology, physical, 89–90, 103; and classification of races, 62; popularized forms of, 62
Anti-clericalism, 26, 67
Anti-colonialism: and the Muslim world, 76; in the late nineteenth century, 64
Anti-colonialists: and Islam, 78; as universalists, 73
Apollo, 7, 12
Apologetics, Muslim, 78, 106
Arabian Nights (Galland), 44
Arabic, language: and Council of Vienne, 29; and Volney, 51
Arabic translations: of lost classical works, 12, 31; in Spain, 14
Arabism, 31
Arabs: and classical Western

authors, 31; West considers a nonentity, 36; seen as Europe's teachers, 53
Archaelogy, 101
Ariosto, Ludovico, 38
Aristotle: and Gerard of Cremona, 16; West's knowledge of, 15
Arkoun, M., 107
Arnauld, Antoine, 46
Asiatick Researches, 56
Averroës (Ibn Rushd), 18; and Dante, 29; popularity in Europe of, 30
Avicenna (Ibn Sīna): Dante on, 29; influence in Europe, 15, 16, 30, 41, 42

Bacon, Roger: on Aristotle and Avicenna, 16, 17; stresses contributions of Islam, 29
Baghdad, 10, 26
Bajazet (Racine), 39
Barth, Frederik, 103
Bāyezīd I, 137–38n.74
Bāyezīd II, 33

Bayle, Pierre, 46
Becker, Carl Heinrich, 67, 71
Beckford, William, 50
Bedouins, 7; West's knowledge of, 18, 19
Bernard of Clairvaux, 14
Biblical exegesis: and Arabic studies, 48; and Eastern philology, 42
Bibliothéque Orientale (d'Herbelot), 44
Blunt, W. S., 64
Boniface of Luca, 4
Bopp, Franz, 61
Boulainviliers, Henri de, 47
Bourgeois Gentilhomme, Le (Molière), 39
Brockelmann, Carl, 100
Bruce, James, 49
Burckhardt, T., 107
Byron, Lord George Gordon, 58

Caetani, Leoni, 71, 89
Cagliostro, Alessandro di, 50
Cahen, Claude, 108, 143n.136
Capitalism, 9; influence on research, 56; and West's understanding of Islam, 76
Chansons de geste: depiction of Islam, 12; as source for *Parzival*, 26. *See also* Literature, popular Western
Chardin, Jean, 49
Charles V (king of France), 34
Charles VI (king of France), 137–38n.74
Charles VIII (king of France), 33, 34
Chaucer, Geoffrey, 30
Chomsky, Noam, 96
Christianity: decline of permits more objective view of Islam,

37, 39; triumphs of Europe attributed to, 66; and exoticism, 39; as an ideology, 24; and competing ideologies, 27, 45; and modern view of Islam, 77–78; and Orientalists, 44
Christians: fundamentalists, 79; early image of Islam, 3–7; and Mongols, 28; in Spain, 5
Chronique universelle (Godfrey of Viterbo), 19
Classical civilizations: study of in West, 61; seen as superior, 91
Classical studies: popularity of, 66; scholarship expands beyond, 85
Classicism: German reaction against, 53–54
Collège de France, 43
Colonialism, 115; in the Middle East, 60, 64, 80; and ethnographic research, 103; and Edward Said's interpretation of Orientalism, 131n.2
Commerce: and influence on the West's image of the East, 19, 21, 23, 31. *See also* Italian commerical cities
Communism, 9; and view of the Muslim world, 74, 75; and Sultan Galiev, 75
Commynes, Philippe de, 34
Comte, Auguste, 87
Conservatism, 119, 120
Constantinople, 32, 33, 37
Conversion, to Islam, 73, 77, 107
Corbin, Henry, 106–7
Cornielle, Pierre, 39
Council of Clermont, 24
Council of Vienne, 29

Critical approach, to primary sources, 94

Crusades, 7, 29, 31; create image of Islam, 10; and respect for Muslims, 21, 22

Culturalism, 102

Daniel, Norman, 35, 78

Dante, 29, 35

Das Leben und die Lehre Des Mohammed (Sprenger), 70

Decline of the West, The (Spengler), 72

Deism, 47

Delacroix, Ferdinand Victor Eugène, 58

Der Stricker, 12

Description de l'Égypte, 51

Devision de la terre de oultremer, 10

Die religiös-politischen Oppositionsparteien im alten Islam (Wellhausen), 71

Diez, Friedrich, 58

Diplomats, Western: impressions of the Muslim world, 9, 10, 63

Doutté, Edmond, 69

Dozy, Reinhardt, 70

Dragoman, 56, 141n.117

East Is West (Stark), 76

Eastern Europe: trends in Islamic Orientalism, 109–11

d'Eckstein, Nicholas, 58

École des langues orientales, 56

Economic history: and recent scholarship, 79, 108; first Islamists' conference on, 143-n.136

Elizabeth I (queen of England), 34

Eroticism: and Islam, 49

Erpe, Thomas van (Erpenius), 42, 43

Esotericism, 73, 74, 107

Essentialism, 80, 91, 92, 120, 121, 127

Ethnography, 69, 103

Eulogius of Cordova, 6

Eurocentrism: decline of, 71, 93; in the eighteenth century, 65; in the nineteenth century, 64–65, 90–91

Europe: as seen by Eastern courts, 42–43; develops critical approach in research, 94; fragmentation of, 6, 29; ideological pluralism in, 42; and images of Islam, 8, 13, 37–38, 59; ideological importance of Islam declines for, 30, 35; Oriental studies spread in, 43; and the Ottoman Empire, 31, 32–33; and nationalistic challenges, 71–72; position of scholarship in, 84, 95; assumed superiority of, 91. *See also* Christianity; Colonialism; Crusades; Islam

Exoticism, 50, 58, 63; first cases of, 38; in eighteenth century, 39; and T. E. Lawrence, 73; and Pierre Loti, 73; in nineteenth century, 52

Factual history (*histoire événementielle*), 88, 100

Fanaticism, in East, supposed, 72, 74

Fascination de l'Islam, La (Rodinson), xi

Foucault, Michel, 85

Fouinet, Ernest, 58

Francis I (king of France), 34
Franks, 4
Frederick II (Holy Roman Emperor), 25
Fundgruben des Orients, 56

Galiev, Sultan, 75
Galland, Antoine, 44, 50
Gardet, Louis, 105
Geoffrey of Bouillon, 7–8
Gerard of Cremona, 15–16
Gerbert of Aurillac, 12
Germain, Jean, 32
Giaour, 59, 141n.120
Gibbon, Edward, 48
Gilson, Étienne, 18
Godfrey of Viterbo, 19
Goethe, Johann Wolfgang von, 53, 58
Golius, Jacob, 43
Gregory IX (pope), 25
Grimme, Herbert, 70
Grunebaum, Gustave von, 102
Guénon, René, 73, 107
Guibert of Nogent, 11

Haly ('Alī ibn al-'Abbas), 30
Hammer-Purgstall, Joseph von, 56
Harff, Arnold von, 37
Hartmann, Martin, 89
Heine, Heinrich, 59
Henry IV (king of England), 6
Henry VIII (king of England), 33
d'Herbelot, Barthélemy, 44
Herder, Johann, 53
Histoire événementielle. See Factual history
Historia Arabum (Ximénez), 19
Historia Ecclesiastica Gentis Anglorum (Venerable Bede), 4

Historians, Orientalist, 69–71
Historicism, 95, 124
History: in Oriental studies, 69; of institutions, 102; literary, 104; of religions, 61, 62, 89, 90; of sciences, 102. *See also* Economic history; Social history
History of the Saracens (Ockley), 48
Homo islamicus, 60
Hope, Thomas, 49
Hugh of Cluny, 6
Hugo, Victor, 58, 59
Human sciences: emergence of 42, 58, 68; taken up by Orientalists, 79; in nineteenth century, 85
Hurgronje, Snouck, 67

Ibn Khaldun, 124
Ibn Māsawayh. *See* Mesuë
Ibn Rushd. *See* Averroës
Ibn Sīna. *See* Avicenna
Ideology: pluralism of in Europe, 42, 44; and scholarship, 40. *See also* Christianity; Nationalist ideologies
'Imād-al-Din Zangī, 23
Imperialism: in the nineteeth century, 53; and the West's image of the East, 64
India, 36, 51, 52
Irrationalism, 104, 105
Islam: Russian communists' view of, 75; misfortunes of the East ascribed to, 66; and Mongols, 27; presumed satanic foundations of, 66; and sexual attitudes ascribed by West, 49; seen as a united force by the West, 8, 67; the West views

more sympathetically, 45, 46–47, 48–49; seen as progressive force, 77; and Vatican II, 77. *See also* Christianity; Conversion; Europe

Islamic studies: traditional isolation of, 109; 113

Islamstudien (Becker), 71

Italian commerical cities, 6–7; 19–20, 21, 35, 137–38n.74

Izutsu, T. 107

Jews: and commercial contacts with Muslims, 19; presumed conspiracy against Church, 66; and Muslim apologetics, 79; in Spain, 13, 30

Jean de Plano Carpini, 28

John of Damascus, 5

John of Segovia, 32

Joinville, Jean de, 10

Jones, Sir William, 51, 52, 53, 56

Journal Asiatique, 56

Journal of the Asiatic Society of Bengal, 56

Journal of the Royal Asiatic Society of Great Britain and Ireland, 56

Kipling, Rudyard, 76

Kītab al-shifā (Avicenna), 16

Koran. *See* Qur'an

Kremer, Alfred von, 70

La Roque, Jean de, 49

Langlès, Louis Mathieu, 54

Languages: in human behavior, 122; study of, 54, 102; teaching of, 103

Lawrence, T. W., 64, 73

Legacy of Islam, The (2d ed.), x

Leibniz, Baron Gottfried Wilhelm von, 47

Lettres Persanes (Montesquieu), 50

Levy Reuban, 108

Lichtenburger, Henri, 53

Linguistics: comparative and historical, 61, 62, 89; and literary history, 104; new methods, in, 102; in nineteeth-century Europe, 95, 96

Literature, popular Western: and Islam, 11–12, 25, 38–39, 67

Loti, Pierre, 73

Louis VI (king of France), 132-n.17

Louis XIV (king of France), 37

Lull, Raymond, 29

Lyautey, Louis Herbert Gonzalve, 64

Mahomet (Voltaire), 53

Mahomet no impostor, or a Defense of Mahomet, 47

Mahomets Gesang (Goethe), 53

Mainet, 8

Marana, Giovanni Paolo, 50

Marlowe, Christopher, 38

Maronites, 42, 51

Martel, Charles, 4

Marxism, theoretical, 74, 127

Massacre at Chios (Delacroix), 58

Massignon, Louis, 64, 77, 78, 106, 108

Maundrell, Henry, 49

Mehmed II, 32

Meninski, Franz, 43

Merchants, European: knowledge of Islam, 21, 37

Merx, Adelbert, 53

Mesuë (Ibn Māsawayh), 30

Methodology, scholarly: ideal, 84; and Comte, 87; philological, 43, 79
Michaelis, Johann David, 48
Middle Ages: image of Islam in, 3–23; 25, 35; later scholars and, 45, 68
Missionaries, Christian, 66
Modernization, of the East: the West's attitude toward, 60, 63, 65, 73, 103
Mohl, Jules, 86–87, 91
Molière, 38
Mongols, 18, 27–28, 29
Monotheism, 28, 77
Montague, Lady Mary Wortley, 49
Montesquieu, Baron de La Brède et de, 48, 50
Moriscos, 40
Moro, Ludovico, 34
Mozarabs, 5, 13
Muhammad, the Prophet: early popular depictions, 11, 12; modern Christian position on, 78; as depicted in the eighteenth century, 48; and Pedro de Alfonso, 13; and Pierre Bayle, 46; and Henri de Boulainviliers, 47; and Goethe, 53; and Godfrey of Viterbo, 19; and Herbert Grimme, 70; and Aloys Sprenger, 70; and Voltaire, 47, 140n.98
Murād III, 35
Muslim world: and anti-colonialism, 76; Communists' view of, 74, 75; Sultan Galiev's views on, 75; theoretical Marxism's view of, 74; viewed as exotic in West, 44. *See also* Islam; Christianity

Nationalism, Eastern: and Sultan Galiev, 75; the West's perception of, 64, 73, 76
Nationalist ideologies: oppose historical spirit, 95, 127
Native scholars. *See* Scholars, native Middle Eastern
Nestorianism, 27–28, 29
New World of Islam, The (Stoddard), 72
Nicholas of Cusa, 32
Niebuhr, Barthold George, 69
Niebuhr, Carsten, 49
Nieuwenhuijze, C. A. O. van, 108, 109
Normans, 6

Ockley, Simon, 48
Onamasticon Arabicum, 100
Oriental studies: Victor Hugo on, 58; regional influence on, 109; negative influences in, 68, 115; isolation of, 82; Jules Mohl on, 86–87, 91; in the Romantic era, 54; impact of WWI on, 71. *See also* Islamic studies; Orientalism; Scholarship, Orientalist
Orientales, Les (Hugo), 58, 59
Orientalism: birth of, 40–41; end of, 81; first use of term, 57; isolation of, 118; and methodology, 86. *See also* Scholarship, Orientalist
Orientalism (Said), 130–31n.2
Orientalists: and Christianity, 44; as conservatives, 44, 96, 98; contentment of, 117; and ideological relativism, 44; influence of Silvestre de Sacy on,

55; skepticism of, 98. *See also* Scholarship, Orientalist

Ottoman Empire: decline of, 59, 64; study of in Europe, 37, 108; as threat to Europe, 31, 32–33, 137–38n.74

Ottoman Turks: seen as Europeans, 35, 36

Oxford University, 43, 48

Pan-Islam: Europe's fear of, 67

Papal authority, 6, 24

Paris: as center of Oriental studies, 41, 43, 51, 54, 68

Parzival (Wolfram), 26, 27

Pedro de Alfonso, 13

Peter the Venerable, 13

Petrach, 31

Philological methods: first text to use, 43; attempts to go beyond, 79

Philology: dominates Oriental studies, 62, 68, 69, 89, 92–93; end of dominance of Oriental studies, 81; in the eighteenth century, 51

Philosophy: and the West's image of Islam, 15, 16, 17

Pilgrimage of Charlemagne, 7

Pluralism, cultural, 95

Pococke, Edward, 43

Pococke, Richard, 49

Poitiers, battle of, 4

Postel, Guillaume, 40 43

Postitivism, 87, 88; retreat from, 71, 106; and textual criticism, 63; and theologians, 104

Prester John, 28

Printing: Arabic script in Europe, 41, 43

Problematics, general, 100–101, 113 122

Qiliç Arslan, 23

Qur'ān, 17; and John of Segovia, 32; and Nicholas of Cusa, 32; and Robert of Ketton, 15; and George Sale, 47; Orientalists' scholarship on questioned, 106

Race: classification of, 90; and cultural essentialism, 80; and Orientalist scholarship, 70

Racine, Jean, 39

Ranke, Leopold von, 69–70

Ravelingen, Frans van, 43

Raymond of Peñafort, Saint, 17

Reconquista, 6, 29

Reductionism, 123

Reiske, Johann Jacob, 48

Reland, Adriaan, 46

Renaissance, the: scholarship in, 31, 38, 41

Renan, Ernest, 55, 142n.123

Rhazes, 30

Rising Tide of Color against White World-Supremacy, The (Stoddard), 72

Robert of Ketton, 14

Roger of Hauteville, 7

Romanticism, 85

Rome: Oriental studies at, 40, 43

Rousseau, Jean-Jacques, 50, 52

Russia: Orientalism in during the nineteenth century, 57

Sacred history, 10–11, 106

Sacy, Silvestre de, 55, 56

Said, Edward, 130–31n.2

Saladin: admired in the West, 22–23, 29, 135n.42, 136n.50

Sale, George, 47

Saracens: the West's image of,

3, 5, 7, 17, 18, 26; term disappears, 36
Saussure, Ferdinand de, 96
Sauvaget, Jean, 101, 143n.136
Savary, Claude-Étienne, 49
Scaliger, Joseph, 41, 43
Schacht, Joseph, x, 102
Schlegel, Friedrich, 54
Scholars, native Middle Eastern: and European scholars, 79, 113; impact on Middle Eastern studies, 93–94; traditionalists' suspicious of, 78, 97
Scholarship, Orientalist: accomplishments of 88; in Eastern Europe, 109–11; first works for general public, 48; in Germany, 56; and the human sciences, 79; first journals, 56; in the nineteenth century, 69–71; and native scholars, 97; dominated by philologists, 68, 89; in Russia, 57; Silvestre de Sacy's influence, 55; Edward Said on, 130–31n.2
Schultens, Albert, 48
Schuon, F., 107
Scientism, 87, 88
Semitic spirit, 67; supposed of Islam, 70, 142n.123
Simon, Richard, 45
Social history, 79, 100, 108
Social sciences, 68, 89
Société Asiatique, 56
Sociology: first studies of Middle East, 68–69; and Orientalists, 93, 98, 108; first Islamists' conference on, 143-n.135
Song of Roland, 7
Southern, R. W., 11, 32

Spain: Arabic studies in, 40; Arabic translation work in, 12–13, 14–15; Islam in, 4, 6; Jews in, 29
Specialization: patronage encourages, 41; and Orientalism, 115, 117; trend toward in the nineteenth century, 56, 62, 85
Spengler, Oswald, 72
Sprenger, Aloys, 70
Stark, Freya, 76
Stoddard, Theodore Lothrop, 72
Structuralist techniques, 122
Studia di storia orientale (Caetani), 71
Suleymān the Magnificent, 34
Summa contra Gentiles (Thomas Aquinas), 17

Tamburlaine (Marlowe), 38
Tasso, Torquato, 38
Tavernier, Jean Baptiste, 49
Tervagant, 7, 12
Textual criticism, 63
Theologians, Christian: attack disciples of Averroës and Avicenna, 17–18; and Ottoman Empire, 31; views on Muhammad, 78
Theologocentrism, 105; defined, 104; and moderate Orientalists, 121; major trends derived from, 105–7
Thomas Aquinas, Saint, 17, 78
Thomas Becket, Saint, 23
Travelers, European: and knowledge of the East, 37, 38, 43, 49

United States, the: scholarly

trends in, ix, 99; and esoterism in, 73, 74

Universalism: and anti-colonialism, 76; reaction against, 85

Vathek (Beckford), 50

Vatican II: on Islam, 77

Venerable Bede, 4

Vie de Mahomet (Boulainviliers), 47

Volksgeister, 61

Volney, Constantin-François de Chasseboeuf, 51, 55

Voltaire, 47, 48, 53, 140n.98

Voyage en Égypte en Syrie (Volney), 51

Weil, Gustav, 70

Wellhausen, Julian, 70

West-östlicher Divan (Goethe), 53

Westermarck, Edward, 69

Westernization: of Eastern literature, 38, 51–50. *See also* Modernization

Willehalm (Wolfram), 26

William de Rubruquis, 29

William of Tyre, 9

Wolfram von Eschenbach, 26

Wycliffe, John, 30

Ximénex, Rodrigo, 19

Zeitschrift der deutschen morgenlandischen Gesellschaft, 56

About the Author

Maxime Rodinson was educated and teaches at the most prestigious institutions of French higher learning known collectively as the Grandes écoles. He has taught Old South Arabian, Old Ethiopic, and Near Eastern anthropology at the École pratique des hautes études.

If Maxime Rodinson has the training of an Orientalist, he is, as he himself puts it, essentially a sociologist and his knowledge of the Middle East includes seven years of residence in Syria, Lebanon, and Egypt. However, Maxime Rodinson cannot simply be considered another sociologist. He was and is committed to what he has called "a militant ethical orientation." As he put it in a interview in *Al-fikr al-Arabi*, he grew up in the anti-colonialist atmosphere of a French Communist household and he recalls participating as a child in rallies supporting the Chinese revolution of 1927 and the Moroccan Rif insurgency during the first half of the 1920s. When most Western scholars saw Arab nationalism as a kind of fanatic aberration, he recognized the legitimate demands for independence in the Arab world.

Much of Maxime Rodinson's scholarly activity has been devoted to the contemporary political practice of the Arab world and to an explication of that practice.

Many of his best known works are in this vein including *Islam and Capitalism* (1966), *Marxism and the Muslim World* (1972), and *The Arabs* (1979). Maxime Rodinson has never been one to retreat from his analyses, even when they led to unpopular conclusions. In 1973 he published *Israel: A Settler-Colonial State*, a seminal scholarly critique of Zionist state-building, which followed up his earlier *Israel and the Arabs* (1968).

These treatments or even topical political concerns do not by any means exhaust Professor Rodinson's research. He has written a widely used biography of the Prophet entitled *Muhammad* (1961) and a scholarly study of magic in Ethiopia, *Magie, médecine, et possession à Gondar* (1967), one of his few books not yet published in English. He has also published articles on medieval Arab cuisine, a subject that has interested him for a long time. His sense of humor and of the realities of the mundane world are apparent in these studies, for as he told one interviewer, not all Muslims shared the identical set of mystical beliefs, but they did all have to eat.

Maxime Rodinson is active in scholarly and other pursuits in Paris. In 1981 he was made a corresponding fellow of the British Academy and in 1985 he became a chevalier of the Legion of Honor in France. Although he has retired from the École pratique des hautes études, he continues to lecture there occasionally and to devote himself to the study of the Middle East. The present volume, *Europe and the Mystique of Islam*, was written as part of his contribution to our understanding not only of the Arab world but of ourselves in relation to it.

Ellis Goldberg
University of Washington